Stamping Hot Potatoes Style

Lush, Plush Projects for the Sophisticated Stamper

Mary Benagh O'Neil

Publisher's Cataloging-in-Publication
(Provided by Quality Books, Inc.)

O'Neil, Mary Benagh.
        Stamping Hot Potatoes style : lush, plush projects for
        the sophisticated stamper / Mary Benagh O'Neil. – 1st ed.
                p. cm.
                LCCN: 2001092463
                ISBN: 0-971116-0-X

        1. Rubber stamp printing. I. Title.

TT867.054 2001   761
                    QBI01-201006

Published by Potato Peel Press
2805 Columbine Place
Nashville, TN 37204
http://www.hotpotatoes.com

Printed in the United States of America

10 9 8 7 6 5 4 3 2 1

Acknowledgments

This list could never be complete, but here goes...
To Karla DesPrez, for tolerating my dreadful procrastination, and even more praise for her design skills; without her this book would be nothing more than a concept. To Tammy Pendergrass for her resolute attention to detail and for being one of the nicest people I've ever known. To Christa Richmond for keeping the potato machine peeling right along without much help or direction. To Mark Jetton for his marketable imagination, his "on a dime turnaround time" and, of course, his more than ample samples. To Vicki MacMahan & Karen Crain Ray for their years of loyal toil in the stamping fields. To Reverend Kay Williams for the Wednesday night inspirational meetings. To the lovely and talented Lynne Krucke. To Carol Duvall for ALL her encouragement and invaluable exposure. To Kelly Ehrlich for standing up for me and sitting on me whenever and whichever the case called for. To Sherry Crain Arledge for years of support, especially during all those rainy craft fairs. To Beverly, Vicki, and all the gals at Textile Fabrics for having the best service and selection right in Nashville, Tennessee. To all the loyal customers who keep my spirit and business alive. To my husband, Brian O'Neil, for providing me with a last name that people can pronounce. And finally to my mother, Christine Benagh, whose editing skills make me look like I can really write and more importantly for nurturing in me and my siblings the notion that we could and can do whatever we wanted to in life.

Contents

Paper

Holiday

Hello

What can I say? I'm a lucky girl! My career in fabric stamping began (as so many things in my life have) by accident. I may be offering more information than you need or want, but if you've already bought my book, well ... I think it might be of interest to you to know how Hot Potatoes started.

This story begins on the beaches of North Carolina. Never one to over commit myself, I had only one goal at that point in my life and that was to live at the beach by the time I was 30. So there I was, waiting tables at night and working in a small graphics firm by day. I enjoyed working at the graphics shop because I had always fancied myself as being artistically inclined. Proofreading and attention to detail, however, were not priorities for me, which was a source of deep concern for my boss who was very nice and probably too tolerant. Suffice it to say I was a pretty good waitress!

It was summertime, and yes, the livin' was easy. And then it happened. I didn't mean for it to happen, it just did. A stain. Coffee. Smack dab in the middle of a brand new sweatshirt. What's a girl to do? Well, if the girl in question happens to be an ex-Girl Scout there is only one thing to do, and it has nothing to do with selling enough cookies to buy a new sweatshirt. "CARVE A POTATO" was what the little voice was telling me to do. And that's exactly what I did. First, I went to a local craft store (a current Hot Potato customer) to buy some fabric paint. Then it was off to the grocery to buy the biggest potato I could find. Next, with my rusty but trusty paring knife I began to carve. Without really trying to I carved what to me looked like a very groovy (yes, I said groovy) fish. I started slapping on some fabric paint and stamped all over that sweatshirt with reckless abandon. When I was finished, I was very happy. I had a sweatshirt like nobody had ever seen in Wilmington, North Carolina.

Being the original "Proud Mary," I wore the sweatshirt to work the next day to rave reviews. My boss wanted a shirt with spiders and hourglasses. I was happy to oblige as his patience with me was wearing a bit thin. Soon after, he suggested that I do several designs on T-shirts to hang in the picture window of his shop. He didn't have to ask me twice, and soon people began stopping by the shop wanting to BUY my shirts! Looking back on it now, I think my boss had been looking for a way to tell me that it was time to move on while at the same time avoiding the ugly business of actually having to fire me. Potato printing had opened the door that he was hoping I would march through. So march I did!

Soon I was selling my shirts to shops up and down the beach. Friends would tell me that when they wore one of my shirts, people would strike up conversations with them just to find out where they could get one for themselves. I was on the brink of a career without really knowing it. Finally I had a job that I loved, I was having fun, making money, and perhaps most importantly, people enjoyed my work! As I said before, I'm a lucky girl.

I've since moved on from carving potatoes in my spare room to buying an old house where, with a handful of great employees, I manufacture rubber stamps for the craft industry.

Recently a friend of mine agreed to help answer the phone while I was away from the office. When I returned she told me that I had the best job in the world. She said the phone rings constantly with people telling how much fun they have using their Hot Potato stamps. OK, some days are better than others, and it's been a long and sometimes bumpy road, but I wouldn't trade it for all the potatoes in Idaho.

Enough about me. I hope you enjoy creating the projects in this book. I know I have.

Techniques

The techniques listed in this section are intended to provide a starting place. You should be able to take any of these techniques and adapt them to your own way of doing things and substitute different materials. With time and experimentation you will develop your own unique style. Accept the fact that there will be mistakes and horrible color choices, but try to learn from the mistakes. Everyone has a bad day now and then when nothing seems to turn out right. But then you will have unexpected success with a piece. So keep plodding along; the reward is there.

FABRIC PRINTING

Printing on fabric was the inspiration for Hot Potatoes. So it seems appropriate to devote a fair portion of this book to stamping on fabric. Stamped cards and mail can make your day, but fashion is so much more fun. Printed garments are practical and unique. People will just reach out and touch your clothes, and this can be a good thing if you are new in town!

Minimal preparation is the only way to go. So here it is in black and white: I never prewash my garments. Who made up this rule? You will be wasting valuable creative time and find yourself doing laundry, not art. Usually you will be printing on T-shirts or T-shirt type garments of a similar fabric. Smooth, 100% cotton fabrics work best. Fabrics with too much texture, such as flannel or terrycloth, do not give very rewarding results.

Picking the right stamps is important in fabric stamping. Big, solid stamps that are deeply etched are absolutely essential. The prints made from solid stamps show up clearly and hold up in washing. Little detailed stamps usually do not give strong enough prints on fabric and fade after a wash or two. (Not to mention that fabric paint is difficult to use on them.) When you just must use a detailed stamp there are inkpads that are easier to work with, but they do not have the permanence that the paint does.

Paint can be applied to fabric stamps in many ways. Foam paintbrushes are the easiest and most economical way to apply fabric paint directly to the stamp. They work well and are easy to clean. Bristle brushes can also be used, and you may enjoy the brush-stroke texture that shows in your fabric prints. Experiment with both.

Fabric paint is usually nontoxic. Here's a hint: Read the clean-up instructions. If the product can be cleaned up with soap and water you can be assured that it is nontoxic. These paints are safer for you, safer for your stamps, and of course required in a classroom situation. I highly recommend Jacquard fabric paint. It is safe to use, and does not leave a rough texture on your fabric when dry. The real test of paint is to print something in black and see how well it holds up in the wash. Black should stay black, even after endless washings, and even bleaching. There are glitters and powders that you can add to fabric paint if that is your style. Metallic paints are available and are always being improved. Experiment to find the methods and products that work best for you.

Colors can make or break your design. Paints straight from the jar always cry to be tampered with. The pinks look too gaudy or the yellows too bright. If a color just needs a little touch of something look at a color wheel. Choose the color directly across from the color you are working with. Add just a tiny drop of the color opposite (the complementary color) your chosen color. An example would be adding the smallest drop of purple to yellow. Always add the darker color in small amounts to the lighter color. For instance, if you want to make a pink you will add small amounts of red to white. If you try to add white to red it will take far too much paint and time.

It's almost time to print, but first prepare the printing surface. Surface irregularities affect the way stamps print. If you are printing a T-shirt, insert a piece of Foam Core inside the shirt to protect the side not being printed. The only time you need to prewash your fabric is when the finished fabric will be cut and sewn into clothing, curtains, or cushions. In that case you need to iron the fabric after washing and drying and place it over the Foam Core. The cushion in Foam Core allows you to bear down with pressure when you stamp. The most time-consuming part of stamping a garment is choosing colors and configuring your design. For a design, odd numbers of images, 3 or 5, are always pleasing to the eye. If you are having trouble with your design, try three colors or three stamp designs.

Random placement of your stamps is a fun place to start and makes quite a statement. It may be helpful when you are first learning placement to think of a number 5 playing card. The spacing and placement is easy to do and pleasing to the eye. Freehand placement is not difficult to master and leaves the finished garments with their own unique signature. If you need a bit of assistance, use a heavy black marker and make straight lines on the piece of Foam Core. These lines show through a white T-shirt and give you guidelines to follow.

Practicing on an old garment or paper bag will allow you to test your design. When printing on a T-shirt start on the back to master your technique. If you create a disaster on the back, most likely you will forget just how ridiculous you look from the rear view, and you never know when people are making fun of you behind your back anyway! The most visible place on your garment is the front right below your face. When you print the front of the garment take time to place your images carefully. Make a point not to place your designs on the two main focal points (this instruction is intended for females, figure it out!)

To print, paint the surface of your stamp, taking care to cover the entire surface evenly. Glide the paint on much like you would fingernail polish. Then press the stamp to the fabric with enough pressure to transfer the image. Carefully lift up the stamp. People have a tendency to jerk the stamp away in a quick motion that often leaves splatter marks behind. If your image is too pale, you may need more paint. If you have too much paint on the stamp, there may be blobs or drips. Use your brush to mop up any excess paint that accumulates on the stamp, especially around the edges. Toothpicks are perfect for cleaning out indentions and detailed areas of your stamps. Fabric paint is permanent! So if you drop a stamp or brush and create a disaster, you might find it best not to try to cover the error of your ways. Sometimes it is less obvious if you do not bring extra attention to this. The worst thing you can do is use water to try getting paint out. You wind up with a big, ugly, watery mess.

If you need to touch up an area, use a small bristle brush or cotton swab to dab paint from the foam brush and then carefully touch up. Remember this paint is permanent on your clothes and carpet, so take the necessary precautions. If you get paint on the margins of the stamp or on your wooden mount, you should wipe it clean at once. A Q-tip is a wonderful tool to keep handy for wiping areas on your stamps and for soaking up excess paint. Remember – practice makes perfect, and during this learning phase you may develop some techniques that will inspire you on future projects. There is no limit to the pattern and color combinations you can create.

Printing on sweatshirts takes a little more caution because of the thickness of the fabric. Any extra paint on the margins of the stamp will print, so take care that there is only paint on the printing surface of your stamp. After you have finished printing the fabric, hang it to dry in an area where it will not be handled.

Although heat setting is recommended, this step can usually be omitted. During the early years of Hot Potatoes, the company did not sell rubber stamps but only finished hand-printed garments.

None of these was ever heat set, simply because the instructions on the paint jars were never read! If you feel uneasy about this carefree attitude then you should simply follow the manufacturer's instructions. When printing on T-shirts, let the finished garment dry for 24 hours and then toss it in a hot dryer for 10 minutes. That's it. Think of this paint as a stain. The longer it has to set up, the more permanent it becomes.

If you are printing on heavier cloth such as canvas, you need to apply more pressure during the printing process. After the garment has dried completely, press it on the wrong side with a hot iron.

VELVET EMBOSSING™

Personal note: Before I dare to give instructions for this technique, I have to express my feelings about Velvet Embossing™. This is the most rewarding craft I have ever delved into. I am totally addicted to the satisfaction I get from every impression I make to achieve this rich and luscious fabric. After trying this process with many stamps, I have found that the big solid images are the only way to go. They have much more impact and hold up to dry cleaning.

I had been experimenting with velvet for several years before I was willing to share this with the world. As with many arts and crafts, there seems to be no technique that is really undiscovered, but in my own little world I stumbled upon this in 1995. I found that the foam cushion and glues used to mount Hot Potatoes to the wood are essential in working with velvet. So what I am telling you is that ordinary stamps will not work, unless you do not mind sacrificing the results to the garbage. But with a Hot Potatoes stamp in hand, go have a blast!

Materials:
Big bold Hot Potatoes stamps: Little detailed stamps get lost in the plush velvet. Hot Potatoes are made with special glue that allows them to take the heat process. We can only guarantee this process with our own Hot Potatoes brand.

Velvet: Acetate/rayon is absolutely the best, and I would not use anything else! Silk and rayon work, but are tricky to deal with and often the embossing comes out over time. Avoid nylon, polyester, or washable velvets – the embossing will be a disappointment!

Misting bottle with tap water

Iron: A cheap iron with steam holes just around the edge works great. You want as few steam holes as possible. I have been disappointed with the low heat on craft and travel irons.

Steps:
Lightly mist the wrong side of the fabric. Place the stamp image rubber side up on your work surface or ironing board. Lay the fabric right side down against the stamp image. Now firmly press the iron (set on high or cotton) to the fabric. Count to twenty and lift the iron up carefully. If there is any dampness press again, but never touch or move fabric. Hold the iron over the entire stamp surface and avoid letting the steam holes hit the design areas. They will make an impression as well. To avoid this you can place a press cloth or even tin foil or heavy paper where steam holes might interfere with the design. The Embossed Velvet™ will hold up to dry cleaning!

VELVET APPLIQUE

An interesting technique for Embossed Velvet™ is to create an applique effect with velvet cut-outs. An example of this technique is the Tabletop Overlay on page 63. For this technique you will need:

Materials:
Hot Potatoes rubber stamps
Acetate/rayon velvet
Manicure scissors
Steam-A-Seam2 double-stick iron-on fusible web
Protective paper from the fusible web
Iron (no steam)
Misting bottle with tap water
Lightweight or sheer fabric

Steps:
Use the instructions for Velvet Embossing™ (page 11) with one important amendment. You will attach the Steam-A-Seam2 at the same time that you emboss the velvet. Simply lay the stamp

rubber side up on your work surface and place the velvet right side down on the stamp. Mist with water. Then lay a piece of fusible web on the wrong side of the fabric and a layer of the protective paper (that comes with the Steam-A-Seam2) on top of the webbing. Press the area of the iron without steam holes onto the protective paper for 10 to 20 seconds. This will emboss the image onto your velvet. The webbing will permanently bond to the velvet, making it more stable and also preventing it from fraying. You will want to emboss your images onto the velvet close together to get the most out of your fabric.

After you have embossed the number of images you need, cut out each image using the manicure scissors. Velvet "lint" gets everywhere, so you might want to wear an apron.

Spread out the piece of fabric that you will be attaching the embossed cut-outs to. Be sure to work on an ironing board or protected surface. Arrange the cut-outs right-side up on top of the background fabric in a pattern you like.

The Steam-A-Seam2 that you attached to your embossing has a tacky back so you can arrange your pattern and it will stay put (to a degree) until the final ironing. After creating your pattern, turn to the wrong side carefully, spread the protective paper over each cut-out and hit with the iron for a few seconds until it bonds permanently.

Note: If you are using a traditional fusible web, you will have to lay the cut-outs upside down to figure out the pattern, then spread the fabric over the cut-outs, then the protective paper, and iron it all.

STAMPING WITH BLEACH

Materials:
Hot Potatoes rubber stamps
Cascade Gel with bleach (other cleaners will probably work, but we know this one will)
Natural fabric: linen, silk, cotton, rayon
Foam paintbrush
Small paintbrush
Foam Core
White vinegar
Iron

Steps:

This technique has varied results, depending on the fabric you are trying to bleach out. So be prepared for unique results every time.

This is a case where it is a good idea to prewash your fabric. Dry the fabric and iron. Dip your foam brush into the Cascade Gel and liberally paint the substance onto your stamp. Press to the fabric and watch as the color begins to fade right in front of your eyes.

Let the stamped fabric dry completely and wash in the machine. Add about a cup of vinegar to the water to stop the bleach reaction to your fabric. There are chemicals made specifically to discharge color from fabric, but the cleansing gel is so inexpensive. The gel is diluted enough so that the bleach does not destroy the fibers of your material to the point of disintegration.

STAMPING ON WOOD

You can stamp on almost any surface, and wood is a rewarding one. Wood presents so many variables that trial and error is almost necessary for clean professional results. I have found that stamping on wood requires a smooth unfinished surface. If this is not possible you will need to sand the area you plan to stamp so the paint can grab onto the surface. Acrylic craft paint is perfect for this application. I have also used latex wall paint and even fabric paint.

There are ways to achieve results appropriate for the project you are working on. A less-than-perfect print offers a more primitive look. You may even want to work on rough wood to create this effect. Or you might prefer a clean finished stamp design. Often you can touch up printed areas with a Q-tip to get a more perfect print.

After your stamped surface is dry, you can protect it with a spray polyurethane finish.

CARVING YOUR OWN

If you have purchased this book, that is proof enough that you are interested in stamps. You have probably purchased some stamps already, beginning a collection, and need a nudge to put them all to use. I suggest you start making your own stamps, and simplicity is the key to your first carved stamps. Even if you have no experience in carving, do not let that deter you.

Materials:
A few good-sized potatoes
X-Acto knife
A kitchen paring knife
Pencil and paper
A cutting board or chopping block

Steps:
First decide on a simple design like a star, tree, or a house. You can practice by drawing the design on paper. Cut the potato in half so you have a nice fleshy potato surface as your carving area. Use paper towels to absorb the moisture from the potato. These humble veggies contain tons of starch and a natural dye as well. The starch dries out your hands, and the dye in a potato can make your hands look quite dirty. (I had to overcome this obstacle, and I have learned to accept "working hands.") Use the X-Acto knife as you would a pencil and carve the chosen shape into the potato. Cut down into the potato about an 1/8' to 1/4". Using the paring knife cut away the area of the potato around the design so that it stands free.

Blot the carved potato on the paper towels and you have a stamp! Sometimes you will find that the natural texture from the potato in your design adds interest. I used to carve an elephant stamp almost daily and found the natural texture from the potato made for wonderful wrinkles in his hide. Your potato stamp can be used a lot in one day, and if you want to try to keep it for a second day of printing, you can extend its life by wrapping the clean stamp in damp paper towels and storing it in the refrigerator.

You can use a multitude of different inks for printing with the potato stamps. Any stamp pad will work. If you print with potatoes on fabric you should use fabric paint applied with a brush. Try your potato stamp on brown kraft paper for wonderful gift-wrap. Use just gold or black inkpads for striking results.

If you find that you enjoy carving, you will want something more permanent than potatoes.

Erasers are a perfect carving medium, though they obviously have size restrictions. E-Z Cut and Safety-Kut also offer a great substance for carving and are specifically designed for this purpose. They are available in sizes from several inches to a couple of feet. This stuff was created for school children to use in art classes because the traditional linoleum carving can be hazardous. It is a carver's dream material. You do not even need sharp blades on your carving tools. I like to have an assortment of linoleum carving tools along with my treasured X-Acto. I have used the same X-Acto for close to twenty years now. I do change the blades, but I have a bond with that old knife. I used the same paring knife for years until it became unusable.

When you are ready to try more complicated designs, use tissue paper and a soft lead pencil to trace the design. After tracing your design, turn the tissue paper over so that the pencil marks are against the carving material. Use your thumbnail to rub the design onto the material. The lead design transfers perfectly to the carving material. Now use your X-Acto to carve around positive areas, the ones that should project above the surface. Carving tools are then used to carve away negative space. Exercise some safety measures and always carve away from yourself. In carving out space, follow the direction of the image. These carving lines often show up in the printing process and become as much of the design as the bold imagery.

Some practice will teach you to manage the positive and negative areas. There is no true right or wrong, but when you do make mistakes they are often fixable. If you enjoy carving your own stamps on any material you will begin to develop your own style.

If you choose to make a stamp that outlines your design, be sure to leave a stamping surface wide enough to give a bold image. Try carving or making prints with different objects. A dinner fork makes an interesting design. A cross section of broccoli makes a wonderful tree. Carve with a ballpoint pen into Styrofoam trays from the grocery. A baby's hand or footprint is one of the most treasured stamp impressions. In fact an early type of stamp was a fisted hand, inked on the heel and used on ancient documents. The print looks very much like a paisley design and may have been the origin of such.

I don't recommend embossing velvet with potato or hand carved stamps.

Materials for Rubber Stamping

Another wonderful aspect of rubber stamping is all the material and accessories that you accumulate as your interests broaden. The marketplace today is filled with so many supplies: powders, glues, inks, paints, and glitters, that it is almost a sport to try to acquire as much as possible. The most essential item is the stamp itself. As I've said before, there are thousands of designs available for every interest. In the source section a few of my

favorites are listed, but goodness knows there are many more. Stamps can be very detailed images of familiar objects or images of licensed characters like Mickey Mouse. Learning sets and alphabets have been around forever. Big solid stamps offer a completely different look. Stamps today are often beautifully mounted on maple blocks with their image indexed on the back.

Stamps are available at specialty stores devoted entirely to this craft. Of course you may buy them via the web and in craft stores. If you are fortunate enough to find a specialty store in your area (always check the yellow pages) patronize them. These stores are committed to rubber stamping and are a valuable creative resource. Stamps are also found in so many styles. There are very small children's stamps that usually have foam backs. Large foam stamps are available for fabric and home décor. You can even find the rubber dies unmounted to make yourself. These are a bargain, but I never get around to mounting them so I don't buy many unmounted stamps. My favorite is the wood mounted variety. Rubber stamps are just wonderful things to own and collect.

Adhesives
Once again the market is flooded with a variety of adhesives. My personal preference for working on paper is Yes glue that reminds me of a big tub of school glue. There is another little tub of glue called Coccoina. The tin that it comes in is so cute; it has its own little applicator brush, and it smells of almonds. And would you believe it is made from potatoes! Any glue called archival, bookbinder, or PVA is well suited for paper.

Spray mount is an alternative to brushing glue on. You need to use it in a well-ventilated area.

Bleaching Materials

You can use commercial cleaners to remove color from fabric. Products like Cascade Gel with bleach and Soft Scrub can be painted directly onto a stamp. When applied to most natural fabrics and papers, they remove the color. We have all splattered these cleaners on our bathrobes while doing domestic chores, so why not create a positive result from a dreary accident? The cleaners seem to have the bleach content diluted enough not to harm the fibers of the fabric or paper.

Carving Material

E-Z Cut, Soft-Kut, or Safety-Kut are brand names for a soft substance that you can carve your own stamps from. Most art supply companies carry something like this. It is very easy to work with.

Cleaners

Sigh. I have to get personal here. This is the department I enjoy the least. I think that a stamp collection that is too clean is the sign of an idle mind. But I suppose that I need to cover at least what I have heard about cleaning stamps. There are lots of stamp cleaners available that you put on your stamps. These tend to be a bit on the costly side. I will use these cleaners if they are handy, but often I wash my stamps under running water and scrub with a fingernail brush. Some folks really frown on my cleaning ways, and I am the first to confess that this is an area I do not worry about. The way I see it, rubber stamps are tools. A good worn tool is a wonderful thing. I like to compare it to an old worn butcher block or a seasoned cast iron skillet. Clean tools are important, but if you never use your tools they are no good at all.

Embossing Guns

Go ahead. Buy this immediately. Every rubber stamping devotee has at least one. These heat tools are available wherever stamp supplies are sold. Embossing guns are essential for success with embossing powders.

Embossing Powders

Here is a wonderful little accessory that will make a true convert out of you if you have never used it before. Sprinkle these powders over a stamped image and heat with a special heat gun, called an embossing gun. The powder makes an embossed image and is just a bit like magic. Glitter of every color is available. (After buying more than I will ever use, I have found that clear, black, and metallic are the most satisfactory.) Embossing pads are available, but pigment inkpads do the job too.

Fabric Markers

These pens are designed for drawing or doing detail work on fabric. It takes several days of air drying and still needs to be heat set to be colorfast. I recommend throwing your project in a hot dryer and ironing on the wrong side as well.

Fabric Pads

These very juicy inkpads are intended for stamping on fabric. I had never had good results until Dr. Martin's fabric inkpads came out. The advantage in using fabric pads is that your prints are more perfect. Many stampers have no tolerance for imperfection. The disadvantage is that you cannot mix and blend colors easily, as it is more difficult to have several colors on one stamp.

Another interesting product is Cut n' Dry from Ranger Ink. These pads let you create your own inkpads by pouring the fabric paint directly onto the Cut n' Dry pad. I was very skeptical but have been pleased with the results. The advantage here is that you can create a multicolor pad and use it for fabric stamping with very clean results.

Fabric Paints

New paints seem to be cropping up every day. I like nontoxic water-based fabric paints like Jacquard and Deka. The finished product is smooth to touch and the colors last and are brilliant.

When choosing fabric paint, test black paint. If it holds up in the wash and stays a true black, then you probably have a good paint.

Foam Core

Available in any office supply store, this board resembles 2 pieces of poster board sandwiching a thin layer of Styrofoam. It is indispensable for fabric stamping. Placed inside a garment it keeps the paint from bleeding through, and the cushion helps in the actual printing.

Hot Potatoes Rubber Stamps

Bold graphic rubber stamps, designed specifically for fabric stamping. The original Hot Potatoes then proved to be perfect for Velvet Embossing™ and is the only brand guaranteed to hold up to Velvet Embossing™.

Inkpads

Inkpads are the next essential tool, but you must have more than one inkpad. There are a variety of pads in many colors for many uses. Of course, a black pad of any type is mandatory.

Permanent Inkpads

The permanent inks are essential if you want to stamp an image that will be colored in. The permanent inks insure that the stamped ink will not run even if you want to watercolor or use water-based markers. Inkpads are available in a multitude of colors. Start with the basics like black and brown. Then as you need colored inkpads add them to your collection. Store these inkpads upside down.

Pigment Inkpads

Pigment pads are more moist than conventional stamp pads. They should be used on porous uncoated papers or they will never dry. Pigments can be used on glossy coated paper if you emboss over the ink. These pigment colors do not fade as quickly as other inks tend to do. Pigment pads are available in several sizes, and there are even rainbow pads. The colors stay separate in the rainbow pads and offer endless possibilities. These pads, like any others, can be re-inked with little bottles of pigment color from the manufacturer. Usually the surface of pigment pads is slightly raised so that you can ink even very large stamps by placing the stamp rubber side up and evenly patting the pad surface across the entire area of the stamp.

Resist Inkpads

These inkpads are made with a material that leaves the stamped image impervious to other inks. You can then color all over and around your stamped areas and they are not affected by the addition of other inks.

Water-based Inkpads

These inkpads come in a huge array of colors. Water-based inks will fade quicker than pigment or permanent inks, so avoid putting your work into direct sunlight. Washable inkpads are excellent for children to use.

Markers and Pencils

Colored pencils are often used to color in detailed images after they have been stamped. There are many brands available, and certain varieties may be used to watercolor as well.

The common markers used in rubber stamping are big, bold, juicy markers. I like Marvy Markers because they have big juicy tips that are good for coloring large solid stamps. The ink stays wet longer, and if you huff on them before stamping it adds a bit more moisture for vibrant coloring. Marvy Markers have inkpads that match each marker color perfectly. Tombo is another brand that I like a lot because the colors blend so nicely. So I urge you to go ahead and buy both! Colored pencils and markers can be more useful than lots of colored inkpads.

Paintbrushes

Foam brushes, often called disposable brushes, are perfect for fabric stamping. I strongly recommend having a separate brush for every color. Artist brushes are perfect for painting in details. These brushes can be extremely expensive so take good care of them.

Papers

The variety of papers available is never-ending. Just touching and seeing some of the handmade papers made here and in the orient can create an addiction. Beautiful papers also intensify your ever-growing stamp habit. I recommend starting with more common smooth papers. There is a huge demand in the craft market for acid-free products. I think most of this is hype. Once you are comfortable with your stamping skills and want to preserve pieces of art you should use archival papers that do not fade. But for most projects choose your papers for the color and texture that you find appealing.

I am partial to uncoated papers that I can use any inkpads on. The smoother the paper the better the stamped impression will be. Some of the lacy textured and coarser papers are more appropriate for background and collage work.

Glossy papers are very popular and show inkpad colors most vibrantly. These papers have a slower drying time, and since I have a tendency to smudge them, I rarely use glossy paper. Pigment inks will not dry on glossy paper unless they are embossed.

It is a good idea to save little scraps of your papers even when you have made mistakes. These scraps can be just the needed element in collages.

Polyurethane Spray

This spray is available at any hardware store. Use it as a protective finish over any wood project after painting and stamping. Polyurethane comes in matte or glossy finishes.

Red Line Tape

This is a the mother of all double-stick tape. (One girl in my office does not know how she lived without it. She could probably be the spokesperson for this stuff.) It goes by several different names, but it always has the same distinguishing red backing. It is available in many widths. It could be used in place of Res-Q Tape.

Res-Q Tape

If you are going to sew with velvet, this product is essential. It is a type of double-stick tape that is used in lieu of basting fabrics together. Velvet slips and slides and can drive you close to insane, so USE THIS! It is also a time-saver. You will usually be putting two right sides of fabric together and the Res-Q Tape goes into the seam allowance. You do not want to sew through it as it makes your needle sticky. It cannot be reused.

Resist Paper

Hot Potatoes Resist Papers have designs preprinted on them with a resist ink. The designs coordinate with many of our stamp images and are fun to use to make cards. Often the designs are barely visible to the eye until water-based inks are applied to the paper. The designs just pop out like magic. I recommend wiping a paper towel over the paper after ink has been applied to remove any excess ink. These papers can take several minutes to dry.

Stamp Positioner

Trial and error may be fine for some, but others may prefer a wonderful precision tool called a stamp positioner. There are many varieties out there, but they all work basically the same way. All have an L or T shaped piece and a piece of tracing paper or plastic that fits into the corner of the L. The tracing paper can be used every time you stamp a particular image while the plastic can be wiped clean and reused for other images.

Steam-A-Seam2

Another essential! This is a fusible web, but it is double-sided. I have found it is a real time-saver when doing velvet cut-outs (see curtain project or tabletop overlay). The slightly tacky backside enables you to have a temporary placement of your cut-outs.

Therm O Web Iron-On Vinyl

Follow the manufacturers instructions to iron this onto fabric or paper. The vinyl makes any surface water resistant. When used on fabric it looks like Mexican oilcloth. Very funky. Very cool.

Tile Stamp Kit

Hot Potatoes offers a kit of precut foam pieces that are the same size as traditional tile. The kit includes five stamps to create the look of 1" and 4' tiles. This faux look can really be fun on walls, boxes, and floors.

Velvet

When it comes to velvet, acetate/rayon is the only velvet! Our high quality velvet produces superior results when embossed with Hot Potatoes rubber stamps. The acetate actually burns into a permanent shining reverse brocade. Acetate/rayon velvet should be dry-cleaned. This fabric is usually available 47" wide. Hot Potatoes carries a wide range of colors. This fabric can often be found in fabric stores, just be sure you are getting the right fabric (acetate/rayon) content.

Velvet Ornament Kit

Make three gorgeous bell-shaped ornaments. Scored patterns are included to make this project a snap. This kit has everything but glue, ribbon, and a stamp.

Velvet Ribbon

We searched the world over for acetate/rayon velvet ribbon. No one made it anywhere, so we did it ourselves. This ribbon matches our yardage of acetate/rayon velvet perfectly. It comes 2", 3", or 4" wide. It is available in 1- and 5-yard lengths. Our ribbon is wired, but the wire can easily be removed. This ribbon is perfect for adding to the hem of jeans or curtains, making purses or pillows, or decorating a mantle or Christmas tree.

White Tulle Wrap and Velvet Purse

Materials - Tulle Wrap:

Hot Potatoes rubber stamp
(2/3) yard of white tulle (70" wide)
(1/2) yard white acetate/rayon velvet
Steam-A-Seam2 double-stick iron-on fusible web
Protective paper from the fusible web
Manicure scissors
Iron (no steam)
Misting bottle with tap water

Steps:

1. Follow the instructions on page 11 for stamping on velvet with one important amendment. Attach the Steam-A-Seam2 at the same time that you emboss the velvet. Simply place the stamp rubber side up on an ironing board, and place the velvet right side down on the stamp. Mist with water. Then lay a piece of fusible web on the wrong side of the fabric, with a layer of protective paper on top of the webbing. Press the area of the iron without steam holes onto the protective paper for 10 to 20 seconds. This will emboss the image of the rose onto your velvet. The webbing will permanently bond to the velvet, making it more stable and also preventing it from fraying.

2. Emboss about 40 roses on the white velvet. Cut out all the roses, leaving a small edge of the unembossed velvet as the border for each piece. This is the most time consuming part of the project.

3. Spread out the piece of tulle on your work surface. Place the roses on the tulle to determine your pattern. Steam-A-Seam2 has a tacky back so you can arrange your pattern and it stays put (to a degree) until the final ironing. If you are using an ordinary fusible web, you will have to lay the roses out upside down to figure out the pattern, then spread the tulle over the roses, then the protective paper and iron it all. Try your best to find Steam-A-Seam2. It makes all the difference in the world.

4. Carefully turn over the entire piece. Be sure you are working on a protected work surface or ironing board. Spread the protective paper over the entire project and iron over each rose, securing it permanently to the tulle. Work with small areas at a time because once the roses have bonded to the tulle they cannot be removed.

Hot Potatoes stamp used: Outline Rose #J250

Materials - Velvet Purse:

Hot Potatoes rubber stamp
(2) 7" x 11" pieces of white acetate/rayon velvet
(2) 7" x 11" pieces of white lining fabric, such as silk or satin
(1) 12" piece of white beading
(1) 12" piece of white marabou
White tassel
(1) yard of white cording or ribbon for purse strap
Iron (no steam)
Misting bottle with tap water
Scissors
Needle
White thread
Sewing machine

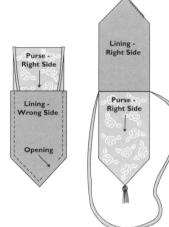

Steps:

1. To form the point at the bottom of the purse, first find the center point of a short side of the velvet rectangle. Next, measure up 2" from the bottom on each long side of the rectangle and mark these side points. Then draw diagonal lines from the center point to each of your 2" marks. Trim off excess fabric to form a point. Repeat for the lining.

2. Emboss the velvet in a random pattern on the front and back pieces of the purse. (See page 11 for Velvet Embossing™ instructions.)

3. Tack the top of the tassel to the bottom point of the right side of the front panel of the purse. (The bottom of the tassel should be pointed up towards the top of the purse.)

4. Sew all sides of the purse except the top, with right sides facing. Make sure the tassel is still pointing to the top of the purse and not sticking out of the seam. Repeat for the lining, but leave a 2" opening in one of the bottom seams.

5. Tack the cording for the purse strap to the top edges of the purse with the cording facing in.

6. Turn the purse fabric right side out. Slip the purse into the lining, keeping the lining right sides together. Sew the purse to the lining around the top edges. Pull the purse and strap through the opening in the lining and slipstitch the opening to finish. (See example above.)

7. Slipstitch beading and marabou around the top of the purse to finish.

Hot Potatoes stamp used: Outline Rose #J250

Stamped Pajamas

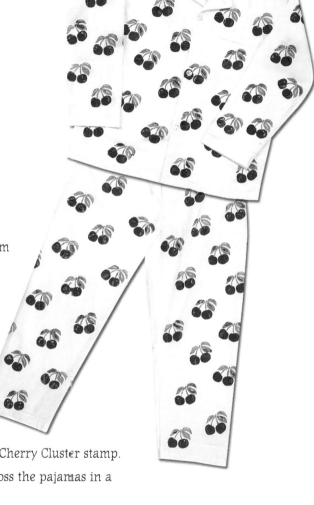

Materials:

Hot Potatoes rubber stamp
Fabric paints in desired colors
100% cotton pajamas, white or neutral-colored
Foam paintbrushes
Artist paintbrush
Foam Core
Q-tips

Steps:

1. Iron the pajamas.

2. Insert the Foam Core into the pajamas before stamping to keep the paints from bleeding through.

3. See page 8 for fabric stamping instructions. Using a foam brush, apply paint to the stamp. Consider the light and shadow that might be on a piece of fruit and experiment with color. A small flash of dark blue as a shadow adds an artistic touch. You can achieve this effect by painting a stroke of dark blue across the cherries.

4. Randomly print the pajamas with the Cherry Cluster stamp.

5. After the paint has dried completely, toss the pajamas in a hot dryer for 20 minutes to heat set.

TIPS: You do not have to prewash any garments before printing. Keep Q-tips on hand to dab up extra paint that may get on the margins of the stamp. This keeps your hands clean. Q-tips are also handy to touch up any spots that may not have printed perfectly.

Hot Potatoes stamp used: Cherry Cluster #N408

Jacquard fabric paints used: Turquoise #JAC114, Ruby Red #JAC107, Emerald Green #JAC117, Sapphire Blue #JAC112, White #JAC123

Velvet Hat & Scarf

Steps - Velvet Hat:

1. Cut cobalt velvet into 3 pieces:*
   Piece 1 - 27" x 5", Piece 2 - 27" x 3", Piece 3 - 9" circle

2. Cut teal velvet into 3 pieces:
   Piece 4 - 27" x 4-1/2", Piece 5 - 27" x 3-1/2",
   Piece 6 - 9" circle

3. Emboss the cobalt velvet pieces with the Feather Leaf stamp. Emboss the teal velvet pieces with the Curly Leaf stamp. (See page 11 for Velvet Embossing™ instructions.)

4. With right sides facing, stitch the ends of cobalt Piece 1 together. Then, pin the cobalt circle to the upper edge of cobalt Piece 1, with right sides facing. Stitch to form the basic hat. (Example 1)

5. Stitch cobalt Piece 2 to teal Piece 5 lengthwise, with right sides together, forming 1 long piece. Next, stitch the ends of the 2 pieces together. (Example 2) Turn the sides together at the roll line, and stitch the edges together. (Example 3) Pin this piece to the lower edge of the hat and stitch. (Example 4)

6. Repeat Step 4 using teal Piece 4 and the teal circle, but leave a 2" opening in the stitching. This forms the "lining" for the reversible hat. Slip it over the basic hat, with right sides together. Stitch across the bottom to join. (Example 5)

7. Turn the hat right side out through the opening. Slipstitch the opening.

* These instructions are for a hat 23" around. Adapt to fit your own size before cutting the velvet.

NOTE: This amount of velvet will actually make 2 hats, but you need this much to get the length for the band and facing.

Hot Potatoes stamps used: Feather Leaf #J392 and Curly Leaf #I393

Materials - Velvet Hat:

Hot Potatoes rubber stamps
(3/4) yard cobalt blue acetate/rayon velvet
(3/4) yard teal acetate/rayon velvet
Iron (no steam)
Misting bottle with tap water
Scissors
Needle
Blue thread
Sewing machine
Straight pins

Ex. 1

Ex. 2

Ex. 3

Ex. 4

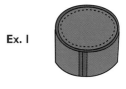

Ex. 5

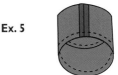

Materials - Velvet Scarf:

Hot Potatoes rubber stamps
(1/8) yard cobalt blue acetate/rayon velvet
(1/2) yard teal acetate/rayon velvet
(1/2) yard lining fabric
(1/2) yard beaded trim
Res-Q Tape
Scissors
Blue thread
Sewing machine
Iron (no steam)
Misting bottle with tap water
Needle

Finished size 8-1/2" x 88"

Steps - Velvet Scarf:

1. Cut teal velvet into (2) 9" x 40" pieces.

2. Cut cobalt velvet into (2) 9" x 3" pieces.

3. Cut lining into (2) 9" x 42-1/2" pieces.

4. Emboss the cobalt velvet pieces with the Curly Leaf stamp. Emboss the teal velvet pieces with the Feather Leaf stamp. (See page 11 for Velvet Embossing™ instructions.)

5. With right sides facing, sew 1 cobalt velvet piece to 1 teal velvet piece on the 9" end. Repeat with the other pieces.

6. Sew the remaining 2 short ends of the teal velvet together with right sides facing.

7. Sew the beaded fringe on the right side at each end of the scarf, with the beads facing in toward the center of the scarf.

8. With right sides facing, sew both of the 9" edges of the lining together.

9. Apply Res-Q Tape to the 4 edges on the right side of the velvet. Peel the paper off the tape to expose the other sticky side. Lay the lining on the velvet with right sides facing, making sure to line up all the edges.

10. Sew the lining to the velvet on all 4 sides, leaving a 2" opening. Make sure the stitching is inside the Res-Q Tape, so that the tape is within the seam allowance. Once the stitching is done, remove the Res-Q Tape.

11. Turn the scarf right side out and slipstitch the opening.

Hot Potatoes stamps used: Feather Leaf #J392 and Curly Leaf #I393

Parade of Animals T-Shirt

Materials:

Hot Potatoes rubber stamps
100% cotton long-sleeved T-shirt
Foam Core large enough to fill inside of shirt
Fabric paints in desired colors
Foam paintbrushes
X-Acto knife

Steps:

1. Use the X-Acto knife to cut the Foam Core in pieces to fit snuggly into the shirt. Cut separate pieces to fit into the sleeves. You may find it easier to work on the sleeves after the front is printed.

2. Follow the basic instructions for stamping on fabric on page 8.

3. Begin printing with the top row of violet zebras. The spacing of your stamps on the first two rows determines the set up for the entire shirt. If you have difficulty making straight rows try this tip: Make dark black horizontal lines on the Foam Core. You will be able to see these through the shirt and can use these straight lines as a guide. Print the elephants, giraffes, and rhinos in rows on the front of the shirt.

4. Print the front sides of the sleeves.

5. Allow the front of the shirt and the sleeves to dry. Then turn the shirt over and repeat the entire process on the back.

Hot Potatoes stamps used:
Zebra #I001, Elephant #J002, Giraffe #I003, Rhino #E004*

*This stamp is discontinued, but if you ask nicely we can still make it for you.

Jacquard fabric paints used:
Violet #JAC110, Goldenrod #JAC102, Ruby Red #JAC107, Apple Green #JAC116

Watercolor Sweatshirt

I found a piece of brightly colored tissue paper that intrigued me. I used this technique to try to duplicate the paper and cover up the white space of the sweatshirt. The final colors are pure and vibrant.

Materials:

Hot Potatoes rubber stamps
100% cotton sweatshirt
Fabric paints
Foam Core

Water
Paintbrushes
Masking tape
Patience

Steps:

1. Use the X-Acto knife to cut the Foam Core in pieces to fit snuggly into the shirt. Cut separate pieces to fit into the sleeves. You may find it easier to work on the sleeves after the front is printed.

2. Mask off areas of the sweatshirt, pressing the masking tape down firmly.

3. Thin out a small amount of the fabric paint by mixing it with water. The ratio is approximately 1 part paint to 4 parts water.

4. Place the Foam Core inside the sweatshirt so that the paint doesn't bleed through.

5. Brush the paint into the masked area. Alternate colors to add interest.

6. If you are painting the entire shirt one color, spritz it with water and then apply the paint. This gives an overall watercolor effect.

7. Allow the paint to dry. This may take several hours. Remove the tape. Re-mask over the painted areas and paint in new areas until there is no white space.

8. Sometimes the paint will bleed through the masking tape, resulting in interesting patterns. If you do not like the way the bleed looks, you can always stamp over it.

9. Now you can also stamp designs in the colored areas. Use the standard method for fabric stamping shown on page 8. Allow the paint to dry and then heat set the shirt by throwing it into a hot dryer for 20 minutes. Heat setting is recommended when the paint has been thinned down as in this shirt.

Hot Potatoes stamps used:
Giant Helix #J252, Big Swirl #D051, Strawberry #I148, Uptown Border #I208*, Cherries #I109, Framing Zig #F243*, Daisy #I309, Checkerboard #O144, Lil DeVine #G194, and Jack #F310

*These stamps are discontinued, but if you ask nicely we can still make them for you.

Jacquard fabric paints used:
Goldenrod #JAC102, Ruby Red #JAC107, Turquoise #JAC114, Apple Green #JAC116 mixed with Yellow Ochre #JAC124

Coffee Break T-Shirt

Materials:

Hot Potatoes rubber stamps
100% cotton T-shirt
Fabric paints in desired colors
Foam paintbrushes
Small artist brush
Foam Core
X-Acto knife

Steps:

1. Use the X-Acto knife to cut the Foam Core in pieces to fit snuggly into the shirt. Cut separate pieces to fit into the sleeves. You may find it easier to work on the sleeves after the front is printed.

2. Follow the basic instructions for stamping on fabric on page 8.

3. Begin printing with the top row of checkerboard. The spacing of your stamps on the first row determines the set up for the entire shirt. You may want to practice lining up the Checkerboard stamp on scrap fabric before you tackle the real shirt.

4. Stamp all the coffee cups. An artist brush is a handy tool for painting in the black details of the coffee in the cup. It is best to stamp all of the turquoise cups, wash the stamp, continue with the violet cups, wash the stamp, and finish with the red cups.

5. Finish the front by stamping the small stars.

6. Allow the front of the shirt and the sleeves to dry. Then turn the shirt over and repeat the entire process on the back.

TIP: If you have difficulty making straight rows make dark black horizontal lines on the Foam Core. You will be able to see these through the shirt and can use these straight lines as a guide.

Hot Potatoes stamps used:
Checkerboard #O144, Coffee Cup #G035, Small Star #A048

Jacquard fabric paints used:
Black #JAC122, Ruby Red #JAC107, Turquoise #JAC114, Violet #JAC110, Dark Periwinkle #JAC125

By the Sea T-Shirt

Materials:

Hot Potatoes rubber stamps
100% cotton T-shirt
Foam Core large enough to fill inside of shirt
Fabric paints in desired colors
Foam paintbrushes
X-Acto knife

Steps:

1. Use the X-Acto knife to cut the Foam Core in pieces to fit snuggly into the shirt. Cut separate pieces to fit into the sleeves.

2. Follow the basic instructions for stamping on fabric on page 8. This shirt is randomly printed. Start with your first stamp close to the neckline. Then print the 2 on each shoulder. That will help to establish a random spacing. The Small Star can also be used to fill any areas where spacing is not pleasing to the eye.

3. All of these stamps have 2 or more colors on them. For example, simply paint the inside of the Helix Sun in yellow and then paint the rays turquoise. Stamp. Note that the green and blue paints have white added to them.

4. Stamp a wave border along the bottom of the shirt.

5. Allow the front of the shirt and the sleeves to dry. Then turn the shirt over to repeat the entire process on the back.

Hot Potatoes stamps used:
Helix Sun #Q135, Seahorse #J132, Scallop Shell #G131, Wave #G133, Small Star #A048

Jacquard fabric paints used:
White #JAC123, Sky Blue #JAC111, Turquoise #JAC114, Goldenrod #JAC102, Ruby Red #JAC107

Feng Shui T-Shirt

Materials:

Hot Potatoes rubber stamps
Fabric paints in desired colors
Water to thin paint
100% cotton white T-shirt
Foam paintbrushes
Small artist brush
Foam Core
Masking tape
X-Acto knife

Steps:

1. Use the X-Acto knife to cut the Foam Core in pieces to fit snuggly inside the shirt. Cut smaller pieces to fit in the sleeves.

2. Follow the basic instructions for stamping on fabric on page 8.

3. Mix the background colors by combining some white paint, a small amount of water, and the base color in a dish. The ratio is approximately 1 part water to 3 parts paint. The water simply thins the paint to allow it to spread more easily.

4. Mask off 3 areas as shown on the shirt with masking tape. Brush fabric paints inside the squares, creating 3 colored backgrounds. Allow this to dry. If you are an impatient one, you might want to speed this process with a hairdryer.

5. Stamp the images onto the background areas using the dark periwinkle fabric paint.

6. Dip the artist brush into the same paint and carefully outline the squares. The masking tape will be helpful to keep the lines straight.

7. Allow all the paint to dry before removing the masking tape.

Hot Potatoes stamps used:
Prosperity #I399, Ginkgo #K339, Bamboo #J271, Dragonfly #G039

Jacquard fabric paints used:
Violet #JAC110, Turquoise #JAC114, Orange #JAC103, White #JAC123, Dark Periwinkle #JAC125

Ducky Dress

Materials:

Hot Potatoes rubber stamps
Cute little cotton knit dress (this is not as effective on a big
  ole adult dress), but it's almost impossible to find these
  items in 100% cotton, so go with what you can find
Fabric paints in desired colors
Foam paintbrushes
Small artist paintbrush
Q-tips
Foam Core to fit inside dress
X-Acto knife

It's cute. It's a duck.

Steps:

1. Use the X-Acto knife to cut the Foam Core in pieces to fit somewhat into the dress. Cut separate pieces to fit into the sleeves. If there are lots of gathers, the Foam Core will not fit snugly.

2. Follow the basic instructions for stamping on fabric on page 8.

3. Soften all of these colors by mixing them with white paint. When making pastel colors start with white paint and add small amounts of color a little at a time.

4. This piece is actually made of sweatshirt material and requires a steady hand. Due to the thickness of a sweatshirt, it easily picks up excess paint, so always make sure that the margins around the stamp are clean of any paint. Keep Q-tips handy specifically for this purpose.

5. Stamp the pattern as shown in the example. After the ducks are stamped, use a small artist brush to paint in the details with undiluted yellow paint.

6. Allow the front of the dress to dry. Then turn the dress over and repeat on the back.

Hot Potatoes stamps used:
Rubber Duck #K180, Small Heart #B156, Grass #B151

Jacquard fabric paints used:
Goldenrod #JAC102, Dark Periwinkle #JAC125, Emerald Green #JAC117, White #JAC123

Dragonfly Shirt

Materials:

100% cotton T-shirt
E-Z Cut or Safety-Kut
  (see materials section on page 18)
Linoleum carving tools
Fabric paints in desired colors
Assorted paintbrushes for details
1" foam paintbrush
Foam Core
X-Acto knife

The dragonfly pattern does not have to be this size... but if you work big you will get quite a workout.

Steps:

1. Using the E-Z Cut, follow the instructions on page 15 for carving your own rubber stamps to make the dragonfly stamps. Trace and then carve the 2 dragonfly patterns on page 117. Carve out all the space except the black outlines.

2. Use the X-Acto knife to cut the Foam Core in pieces to fit snuggly into the shirt. Cut separate pieces to fit into the sleeves. You may find it easier to work on the sleeves after the front is printed.

3. Follow the basic instructions on page 8 for stamping on fabric. Stamp the big dragonfly first with black fabric paint. Using black paint stamp the small dragonfly to fill in areas where there is too much white space.

4. Let the black paint dry completely. You will be able to tell if it is dry by simply touching it.

5. Paint in the other colors using the small paintbrushes.

6. Allow the front of the shirt and the sleeves to dry. Then turn the shirt over and repeat the entire process on the back.

Jacquard fabric paints used:
Black #JAC122, Apple Green #JAC116, Emerald Green #JAC117, Goldenrod #JAC102, Sky Blue #JAC111

Oilcloth Purse

Materials:

Hot Potatoes rubber stamps
Fabric paints in desired colors
(1/2) yard white cotton fabric
(1/2) yard contrasting lining fabric
 (I used a pink and white gingham)
Therm O Web iron-on vinyl
 (available at many craft and fabric stores)
(1) yard of 1" cording or webbing for handles
Plastic fruit: grapes, apples, etc.
Hot glue gun (optional)
Iron
Needle
Thread
Scissors
Foam paintbrushes
Sewing machine

Steps:

1. Cut 2 pieces of white cotton fabric - 11" x 13".

2. Cut 2 pieces of contrasting lining fabric - 11" x 13".

3. Using a foam brush, paint the stamps with fabric paint. (See page 8 for fabric stamping instructions.)

4. Stamp the white cotton fabric pieces with a variety of fruit stamps placed randomly.

5. After stamping both pieces of the white fabric, use a foam brush to paint the background between the stamps. Use a mixture of turquoise and white paint and dilute with water (about 50% water to 50% paint). Leave a white border around the stamped images rather than try to get right up to the edges. Allow to dry

6. Follow the directions that come with the Therm O Web vinyl, and iron the vinyl onto the painted fabric pieces.

7. Cut 2 pieces of cording 18" each for the handles. Tack the ends of the handles to the top edge of the purse, with the handles facing down.

8. Put the right sides of the purse together and sew on 3 sides, leaving the top open (11" side). Repeat for the lining.

9. Turn the purse fabric right side out. Slip the purse into the lining, keeping the lining right sides together. Sew the purse to the lining around the top edges, leaving a 2" opening. Turn the purse inside out and slipstitch the opening to finish.

10. Attach plastic fruit to the front of purse with hot glue, or tack it on with a needle and thread.

Hot Potatoes stamps used:
Big Watermelon #T160*, Strawberry #I148, Apple #O175, Pineapple #J110, Pear #J338, Peach #I107*

*These stamps are discontinued, but if you ask nicely we can still make them for you.

Jacquard fabric paints used:
Turquoise #JAC114, Goldenrod #JAC102, Apple Green #JAC116, Orange #JAC103, Ruby Red #JAC107, White #JAC123

Brown Velvet Purse

Materials:

Hot Potatoes rubber stamp
(2) 7" x 11" pieces of brandy acetate/rayon velvet
(2) 7" x 11" pieces of Chinese silk
 (I used a copper color)
(2) 7" pieces of decorative trim and beading
 for the purse front
Beaded tassel
(I) yard of cording or ribbon for purse strap
Iron (no steam)
Misting bottle with tap water
Brown thread
Needle
Scissors
Sewing machine

Steps:

1. To form the point at the bottom of the purse, first find the center point of a short side of the velvet rectangle. Next measure up 2" from the bottom on each long side of the rectangle and mark these side points. Draw diagonal lines from the center point to each of your 2" marks. Trim off excess fabric to form a point. Repeat for the lining.

2. Lay beading and trim on the front of the velvet to determine the placement for the embossed images. Emboss the velvet using selected stamp to emboss the image in 2 rows, leaving 1" at top for seam. (See page 11 for Velvet Embossing™ instructions.)

3. Machine or hand sew the beaded trim in 2 rows to the front of the purse, making sure the trim goes to the edges. Tack the top of the tassel to the bottom point of the right side of the front panel of the purse. (The bottom of the tassel should be pointed up towards the top of the purse.)

4. Sew all sides of the purse except the top, with right sides facing. Make sure the tassel is still pointing to the top of the purse and not sticking out of the seam. Repeat for the lining, but leave a 2" opening in one of the bottom seams.

5. Tack the cording for the strap inside the top edges of the purse.

6. Turn the purse fabric right side out. Slip the purse into the lining, keeping the lining right sides together. Sew the purse to the lining around the top edges. Pull the purse and strap through the opening in the lining. Slipstitch the opening to finish. (See example.)

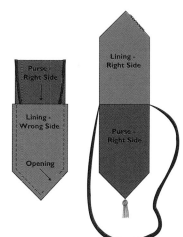

Hot Potatoes stamp used: Tattoo You #1402

Orange Silk Purse

Materials:

Hot Potatoes rubber stamp
(2) 7" x 7" pieces of orange silk
(2) 7" x 7" pieces of contrasting silk for lining
(2) 7" pieces of decorative trim and beading for the purse front
Fabric paint in desired color
Foam paintbrush
(1) yard of cording or ribbon for purse strap
Orange thread
Needle
Sewing machine

Steps:

1. Lay the beading and trim on the front of the silk to determine the placement of the stamped images. Stamp the fabric (see page 8 for fabric stamping instructions), making 1 row of the Square Curl image.

2. Machine or hand sew the beaded trim in 2 rows across the front of the purse, making sure the trim goes to the edges.

3. With right sides facing, stitch 3 sides of the purse, leaving the top open. Repeat on contrasting silk for the lining, but leave a 2" opening in the bottom seam.

4. Tack the cording for the purse strap to the top edges of the purse with the cording facing in.

5. Turn the purse fabric right side out. Slip the purse into the lining, with right sides facing. Sew the purse to the lining around the top edges. Pull the purse and strap through the opening in the lining and slipstitch the opening to finish. (See example.)

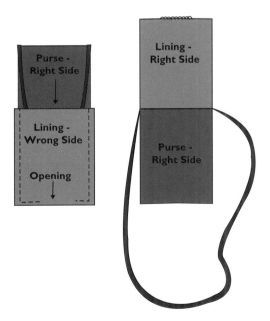

Hot Potatoes stamp used: Square Curl #F358
Jacquard fabric paint used: Ruby Red #JAC107

Mauve Silk and Velvet Purse

Materials:

Hot Potatoes rubber stamp
(1) 7" x 7" piece of mauve acetate/rayon velvet
(2) 2-3/4" x 7" pieces of mauve acetate/rayon velvet for front side panels
(2) 7" x 7" pieces of Chinese silk for lining (I used a light mauve)
(1) 2-1/2" x 7" piece of Chinese silk for front center panel
(2) 7" pieces of decorative trim for the purse front
(1) 7" piece of decorative trim beading for the purse bottom
Fabric paint in desired color
Foam paintbrush
(1) yard of cording or ribbon for purse strap
Iron (no steam)
Misting bottle with tap water
Mauve thread
Needle
Sewing machine
Scissors

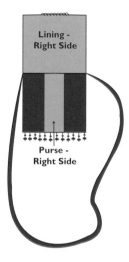

Steps:

1. Stamp the 2-1/2" x 7" piece of Chinese silk for front center panel (see page 8 for fabric stamping instructions), with the DeVine image. Emboss the 2 pieces of mauve acetate/rayon velvet 2-3/4" x 7" for front side panels with the DeVine image. (See page 11 for embossing instructions)

2. With right sides together, stitch 1 velvet panel on either side of the silk panel.

3. Machine or hand sew the beaded trim in 2 rows on either side of the silk panel on the front of the purse, making sure the trim goes to the edges. Sew the beaded trim to the bottom of the purse front, making sure the beads are pointed up towards the top of the purse.

4. With right sides facing, stitch 3 sides of the purse, leaving the top open. Repeat with Chinese silk for the lining, but leave a 2" opening in the bottom seam.

5. Tack the cording for the purse strap to the top edges of the purse with the cording facing in.

6. Turn the purse fabric right side out. Slip the purse into the lining, keeping the lining right sides together. Sew the purse to the lining around the top edges. Pull the purse and strap through the opening in the lining and slipstitch the opening to finish. (See example)

Hot Potatoes stamp used: DeVine #P195

Jacquard fabric paint used: Sapphire Blue #JAC112

Bed Bugs

Materials:

Hot Potatoes rubber stamps
(2) 100% cotton pillowcases
(1) 100% cotton flat sheet
Foam Core
Fabric paints in desired colors
Foam paintbrushes
Fabric markers - all colors from a set of Pebeo SetaSkrib

I love these sheets!! It took some time to color all the detail, but I just took my time and colored while I watched TV. I waited a week or two before I used them so that the markers could really set, and I did heat set them as well by ironing with a very hot iron before the first wash. I want these to last!

Steps:

1. Following the directions on page 8, stamp the bugs on your sheet and pillowcases. Don't forget to insert the Foam Core into the pillowcases and under the sheet before stamping to keep the paints from bleeding through. Stamp the Japanese Beetles in turquoise, the Cicadas in orange and the Skeeters in yellow. Cover the body of the pillowcases with bugs, turning the stamps as you go to create random patterns. Then stamp the opening edges with the three different leaves. Repeat for the second pillowcase and the "turn-down" edge of the flat sheet. Only a glutton for punishment would print the entire top sheet, and you would clearly have to be unstable to stamp the fitted sheet. Choose what you want to do. For this example the obvious and more uncomplicated choice was made.

2. Allow the paint to dry.

3. Use the fabric markers to color in details and dots. Just get carried away. Shading and outlining make for pleasant touches as well.

4. Let the finished pieces cure (sit without washing) for 2 weeks. Markers are not as permanent as one might wish, and this allows them to really set up. Iron any printed areas with a hot iron for the final heat set before washing.

Hot Potatoes stamps used:
Japanese Beetle #L407, Skeeter #L406, Cicada #I419, Feather Leaf #J392, Leaf Trio #L394, Curly Leaf #I393

Jacquard fabric paints used:
Goldenrod #JAC102, Orange #JAC103, Turquoise #JAC114 mixed with White #JAC123, Apple Green #JAC116 mixed with Yellow Ochre #JAC124

Dish Towel

Materials:

Hot Potatoes rubber stamps
100% cotton dish towels ("flour sack" towels are available at discount stores--these are great and inexpensive, but do shrink a lot)
Foam Core, at least as large as dish towels
Fabric paints in desired colors
Foam paintbrushes

Steps:

1. Follow the basic instructions for stamping on fabric on page 8 to print the various eating utensils randomly around the dish towel. It will save time if all the yellow utensils are printed first. Then print all the red utensils, then green, then blue.

2. Allow to dry.

Hot Potatoes stamps used: Knife #1101, Fork #1102, Spoon #1103

Jacquard fabric paints used:
Goldenrod #JAC102, Sapphire Blue #JAC112, Apple Green #JAC116, Ruby Red #JAC107

Fiesta Napkins

Materials:

Hot Potatoes rubber stamps
Plain 100% cotton napkins
Foam Core, at least as large as unfolded napkin
Fabric paints in desired colors
Foam paintbrushes

Steps:

1. Follow the basic instructions for stamping on fabric on page 8 to print the various pitchers around the edges of the napkins. Plan the spacing so that you have an even placement on each border.

2. Fill in with the Wiggle.

3. Allow to dry.

Hot Potatoes stamps used:
Hall Pitcher #1031*, Teapot #L033*, Fiesta Pitcher #J032*, Wiggle #GC47

*These stamps are discontinued, but if you ask nicely we can still make them for you.

Jacquard fabric paints used:
Goldenrod #JAC102, Sapphire Blue #JAC112, Apple Green #JAC116

These instructions are for the pistachio green book cover in the center of the page. To make the other books, substitute ribbon colors or use acetate/rayon velvet yardage in the color of your choice.

Book Covers

Steps:

1. Trace around your open book onto a piece of cardstock adding 2" to the long sides only. These will be your flaps. Cut out the cardstock.

2. Lay the cardstock right side down on your work surface. Place your open book on top of the cardstock and fold the flaps in over the edges of the book. Make sure the book fits with the front and back covers inserted into the flaps. Close and open to be sure there is enough "give." Remove the book.

3. Cut your velvet 1" larger than the cardstock on all 4 sides.

4. Emboss the velvet following the instructions on page 11.

5. Fold the cardstock flaps under and apply spray adhesive to the exposed surface of the cardstock. You may want to mask areas off with Post-it Notes to keep them free of the spray adhesive. If you get a little on the flaps it's okay, but it will be easier if they aren't sticky. You'll have a few minutes before the spray adhesive dries.

6. Place your velvet, right side down, on the work surface and center your sprayed cardstock over it. Gently press down, making sure it sticks. Flip it over and check for wrinkles. If you need to reposition you have some time, just pull up and press back down.

7. Next, cut slits in the velvet margin where the flap folds and also at the end of each flap top and bottom (see diagram below). Using glue or Red Line tape, fold down and stick the velvet margins over the cardstock flaps at the top, creating a pocket on each side for the edges of your book to slide in.

Materials:

Hot Potatoes rubber stamps
Acetate/rayon velvet (enough to wrap around the book, plus 4" each way)
(1/2) yard Hot Potatoes pistachio acetate/rayon velvet
(1/2) yard Hot Potatoes green acetate/rayon velvet ribbon (2")
Daily planner book, calendar, address book, or photo album
Spray adhesive
Glue or Red Line double-stick tape
Cardstock
Scissors
Iron (no steam)
Misting bottle with tap water
(1") piece of Velcro
Post-it Notes

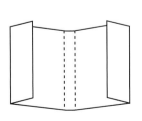
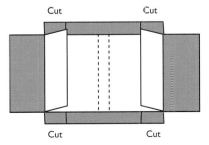
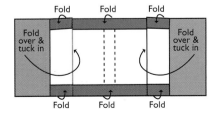

Hot Potatoes stamps used: Outline Puzzle #J349, Solid Puzzle #J348, Curly Curl #N359

8. Glue down remaining velvet margins across top and bottom.

9. Apply a little more glue or Red Line tape to edge of the velvet on each side and wrap around the pocket, tucking the excess inside. Insert your book.

10. Velvet ribbon can be added to keep your book closed. (Hot Potatoes has the only embossable velvet ribbon. Use it.) Remove the wires from each side of the ribbon.

11. Wrap the ribbon around the book to determine length. Add about 3" for an overlap. Apply Red Line double-stick tape to the back of the ribbon in areas where it will touch the book, but no glue or tape should be used where it wraps around the pages. Fold the ends under before sticking and allow for a little overlap. Apply Velcro on the overlapping piece and voila, you're done!

Materials for other book covers

NOTE: All ribbon used is Hot Potatoes acetate/rayon velvet ribbon.

Horizontal striped velvet book:
    Pistachio ribbon (2" wide)
    Teal ribbon (4" wide)
    Cobalt blue ribbon (2" wide)
    Hot Potatoes stamps used: Celtic border #F354, Celtic Groove Thang #L403, Tattoo You #I402

Vertical striped velvet book:
    Red ribbon (3" wide)
    Teal ribbon (2" wide)
    Pistachio ribbon (3" wide)
    Hot Potatoes stamps used: Olive Dots #P421, Small Dots #J420

Teal velvet book:
    Red ribbon (2" wide)
    Hot Potatoes stamps used: Peacock Feather #Q340, Tri-Curl #F357

Cobalt velvet book:
    Hot Potatoes stamps used: Four Point Star #I306, Big Swirl #D051

Pea Clock

Materials:

Hot Potatoes rubber stamps
Cheap clock
Cardstock
Dye-based inkpads in
   rainbows and sclids
Scissors
X-Acto knife

Compass, or pencil
   and a piece of string
Pencil
Post-it Note
Stamp positioner
   (See page 22)
Colored pencils or pens
Jewels

Steps:

1. Buy a cheap battery-operated clock. Make sure that the clear plastic cover is removable (try not to get caught taking it apart by the store clerk).

2. Take apart the clock carefully. Put all the parts in a safe place that you'll remember! The clock face (the part with the numbers) should be either a piece of cardstock or plastic and should come out pretty easily.

3. Use the clock face as a template and trace it (including the center hole) onto a piece of cardstock. If you can't remove it just measure it and draw a circle the same size using that compass you used in geometry class or a pencil on a piece of string.

3. Cut out the circle.

4. Use a pencil to mark off the hours. There should be 12 of them, but if you are pressed for time you can just focus on the 3, 6, 9 and 12.

5. Stamp the Tri-Curl stamp in the center of the circle. Stamp the Tri-Curl stamp again on a Post-it Note. Cut this out and place it over the Tri-Curl on the clock face. This is a mask to protect the Tri-Curl stamp while decorating with the Peacock Feather.

6. Stamp 1 Peacock Feather for each hour. You can drive yourself crazy trying to "eyeball it", but it's usually less stressful to use a stamp positioner. (See materials list for how to use a stamp positioner.) Remember if you really mess it up, just start over on another piece of cardstock.

7. Add extra color as desired with colored pencils or pens. Add jewels.

8. Remember where you put the clock parts and reassemble.

Hot Potatoes stamps used: Tri-Curl #F357 and Peacock Feather #Q340

Bleach Chair

Materials:

Hot Potatoes rubber stamp
Foam paintbrush
Small paintbrush
Household dishwasher cleanser with bleach (I know from experience that Cascade Gel with bleach works well)
(1-2/3) yards (approximately—see Instruction 2 below) natural fabric such as linen, silk, cotton, rayon (I used linen in this example)
Beach chair
Trims for decoration (I used rickrack braid)
Foam Core
Masking tape
Scissors
Thread to match fabric
Sewing machine

Steps:

1. Practice the bleaching technique outlined below on a scrap piece of the fabric until you get the desired effect. Some fabrics work better than others, so a test piece is suggested.

2. Measure to see how much fabric you will need. Usually you will be replacing an existing cover, so just use the same measurements, allowing 1-1/2" on each edge for a hem and several inches on each end to wrap around wooden frame.

3. Mask off vertical lines on the fabric. Leave about an inch between each line of tape to paint your stripes. These can also be painted free hand if you trust yourself in this department.

4. Place Foam Core under your fabric to protect your work surface from the bleach.

5. Load your foam brush with the dishwasher gel or cleanser and paint the lines between the masking tape. The color of the fabric will begin to fade fairly quickly. Because the bleach is diluted in the cleanser, it is not too strong and will not eat the fibers of your piece or damage the stamp. Straight bleach is a disaster and cleansing gel is so inexpensive compared to products made for discharging color. Not to mention that cleansing gel is multifunctional!

6. Remove the tape. The lines will not be perfect. This gives the project an overall batik effect.

7. Apply cleanser to the stamp and print the fabric. Allow to dry.

8. Hem the long edges of the fabric.

9. Sew funky trims on the chair for decoration. We used rickrack braid.

10. Assemble fabric and chair. This particular chair seat is stapled to the chair's wooden frame. Staple fabric on under side of frame, then wrap around once to reduce strain and strengthen.

11. Make a tall cold drink. Put on sunglasses. Collapse.

Hot Potatoes stamp used: Palm #L029

Velvet Ribbon Lampshade

Materials:

Hot Potatoes rubber stamps
(1-1/4) yards teal Hot Potatoes acetate/rayon velvet ribbon (3" wide)*
(1-1/4) yards pistachio Hot Potatoes acetate/rayon velvet ribbon (2 wide)*
(1-1/4) yards ribbon, trim, and beading to coordinate with velvet*
Straight-sided lampshade (this should have as little taper as possible from top to bottom – we used a shade that is 42" in
    diameter at the bottom)
Red Line double-stick tape
Scissors
Iron (no steam)
Misting bottle with tap water

* Or determine yardage needed based on the diameter of the lampshade

Steps:

1. Follow the instructions on page 11 to emboss the velvet ribbon.

2. Apply Red Line double-stick tape to the back of the ribbon
    and the trim. Start in the back of the lampshade where the
    seam already exists and wrap the ribbon and trim pieces
    around the lampshade. Overlap the trim to hide the edges of
    the ribbon.

3. Turn the raw edges of the ribbon under and attach it to the
    shade with another small piece of Red Line tape to form a
    neat seam in the back.

4. Turn the light on from time to time to make sure there are no
    big gaps where the light shines through.

NOTE:
To make the teapot lampshade shown in the inset photo, I used:
(1) yard teal Hot Potatoes acetate/rayon velvet ribbon (3" wide)
(1) yard cobalt blue Hot Potatoes acetate/rayon velvet ribbon (2' wide)
(2) 1 yard pieces of beaded trim
(3) 1 yard pieces of decorative trim

Hot Potatoes rubber stamps used: Tattoo You #1402 and Celtic Groove Thang #L403
Inset photo: Flower Leaf #F240, Cherry Blossom #O398

Tulle Tabletop Overlay

Materials:

Hot Potatoes rubber stamp
(1/3) yard of several colors of acetate/rayon velvet (we used burgundy, green, and brown)
(1) yard tulle
Steam-A-Seam2 double-stick iron-on fusible web
Protective paper from the Steam-A-Seam2 fusible web
Manicure scissors
Scissors
Iron (no steam)
Misting bottle with tap water

Steps:

1. Follow the instructions on page 11 for Velvet Embossing™ with one important amendment. Attach the Steam-A-Seam2 at the same time that you emboss the velvet. Simply place the stamp rubber side up on an ironing board, and place the velvet right side down on the stamp. Mist with water. Then lay a piece of the fusible web on the wrong side of the fabric, with a layer of protective paper on top of the webbing. Press the area of the iron without steam holes onto the protective paper for 10 to 20 seconds. This will emboss the image of the oak leaf onto your velvet. The webbing will permanently bond to the velvet, making it more stable and also preventing it from fraying.

2. Emboss about 25 leaves onto each color of velvet.

3. Cut out all the leaves, leaving a small edge of the unembossed velvet as the border for each leaf.

4. Cut a piece of tulle to the approximate size you want. Spread out the piece of tulle on your work surface. Place the leaves on the tulle to determine your pattern. Steam-A-Seam2 has a tacky back so you can arrange your pattern, and it stays put (to a degree) until the final ironing. If you are using an ordinary fusible web, you will have to lay the leaves out upside down to figure out the pattern, spread the tulle over the patterned leaves, then the protective paper, and iron it all. Try your best to find Steam-A-Seam2. It makes all the difference in the world.

5. Carefully turn over the entire piece. Be sure you are working on a protected work surface or ironing board. Spread the protective paper over the entire project and iron over each leaf, securing it permanently to the tulle. Work with small areas at a time because once the leaves have bonded to the tulle they cannot be removed.

6. Trim tulle around outside edges.

Hot Potatoes stamp used: Open Line Oak Leaf #Q326

Velvet Throw

Materials:

Hot Potatoes rubber stamp
(1-1/2) yards cardinal cross-dye acetate/rayon velvet
(1-1/2) yards lining fabric (because velvet is so luxurious,
   choose a lining that is its equal, such as silk or satin)
Res-Q Tape
(5) yards of fringe
Iron (no steam)
Misting bottle with tap water
Scissors
Needle
Burgundy thread
Sewing machine

My throw at home is larger than this. I had to put a seam down the middle to get it as wide as I wanted. No one has ever noticed! It's lovely!

Steps:

1. Cut velvet and lining into 45" squares.

2. Emboss the velvet with the Peacock Feather stamp. See page 11 for Velvet Embossing™ instructions.

3. Apply Res-Q Tape to the four edges of the right side of the velvet. Peel off the paper on the tape to expose the sticky side. Lay the right side of the lining on the right side of the velvet, making sure to line up all the edges.

4. Sew the 4 sides of the lining to the velvet, leaving a 4" opening. Make sure the stitching is inside of the Res-Q Tape, so that the tape is in the seam allowance. Once the stitching is done, remove the Res-Q Tape.

5. Turn the throw right side out and slipstitch the opening.

6. Machine or hand sew fringe around all four sides of the throw.

7. Curl up on your sofa with a good book and this throw. Fall asleep surrounded by velvet.

Hot Potatoes stamp used: Peacock Feather #Q340

Ginkgo Wooden Box

Materials:

Hot Potatoes rubber stamps
Wooden box
Acrylic paints in green and black
Water to thin paint
Rag or paper towels
(4) wooden balls/knobs
(4) screws (optional)
Twine
Glue
Drill
Spray sealant, such as Krylon Crystal Clear or polyurethane spray
Chinese coin or a decorative button with a hole in the center

Steps:

1. Wait for a sale on an unfinished wood box at your local craft/art store. Don't pay full price for the box unless you're desperate. Save your money for stamps!

2. Water down the green acrylic paint (one part water to one part paint) and spread it all over your box. Wipe it down with a rag or paper towels. Repeat the process until you get the color you want. The more you do it the darker it will be. Let dry.

3. When it is dry to the touch, work up your courage and stamp the Ginkgo in a random pattern with green acrylic paint. If you make a huge mess you can always sand it off or paint over it. Besides, you got the box on sale, right?

4. When all the leaves are dry, carefully stamp the Chinese Love character in the center of the box with black acrylic paint. Then, spacing evenly, stamp the Discovery character on either side of the Love character.

5. Paint the balls or knobs black, and when dry either glue them on or use screws to make them more secure.

6. Spray the entire box with sealant.

7. Add the Chinese coin or button as a clasp. Drill a small hole through the upper lid and thread a loop of twine through the hole. The loop should be just large enough to fit over the coin. Glue into hole. Drill a second hole to attach the coin with another small piece of twine. Take a small piece of twine and fold it in half. Slip the folded end through the center of the coin, pulling through enough twine to loop entirely over the coin. Pull taut. Glue the ends into the drilled hole.

66

Hot Potatoes stamps used: : Ginkgo #K339, Discovery #J345, Love #L344

Tassel Box

Materials:

Hot Potatoes rubber stamps
Unfinished 6" x 6" x 6" wooden box
Acrylic paints in desired colors
Glue
Tacky glue-on jewels
Spray sealant, such as Krylon Crystal Clear
    or polyurethane spray

Steps:

1. Paint box with acrylic paint. Each side of this box is a different color. Put one hand on the inside of the box and paint with the other hand to avoid getting fingerprints of the wrong color on the different sides.

2. After the paint dries stamp the tassels and swags, one side at a time. Pick a contrasting color so the designs will pop out. (It's a good idea to stamp out your design on paper to make sure it will fit and so that you get the look you want.) Fill in the stamped images with the same color. Don't worry if it looks messy at this point!

3. When the paint from Step 2 has dried, stamp over the previously stamped images with a darker contrasting color...I know, it's almost impossible to get it perfect. Keep in mind that the pictured box was made by professionals who get paid the big bucks to be perfect, but you don't have to! If you want, you can deliberately misalign the stamps for an interesting effect (and your self-esteem will be much higher).

4. Stamp the Jacks and let dry.

5. Glue on jewels and spray the finished box with sealant.

Hot Potatoes stamps used: Swag #L273*, Big Tassel #L274 Jack #F310

*This stamp is discontinued, but if you ask nicely we can still make it for you.

Floor Cloth

Materials:

Hot Potatoes rubber stamps
(1) 26" x 36" piece of heavy canvas
White latex house paint
Acrylic paint, house paint, artist paint, etc. (this is a great
    place to use water-based paint you may already have)
Sealant such as Verethane (good because it doesn't yellow)
    or polyurethane
Glue or carpet tape
Masking tape
Foam paintbrushes
Small artist paintbrushes
Pencil
Non-skid mat

Steps:

1. Prime canvas with several coats of white latex paint. Regular house paint works fine and is pretty cheap, but gesso can be used as well.

2. Cut the four corners of the canvas off as shown in Example 1. Fold under the inch wide edge. This will leave you with neat corners. Secure with carpet tape or strong glue.

3. Let the glue dry, and then pencil in your design. Remember that you may have to look at this for a long time, so take time with your design.

4. Using acrylic or latex paint, start filling in your design according to your pencil marks. Usually it is easier to start in the middle. Masking tape is great for making straight lines.

5. After your paint dries, break out the stamps! Simply use the foam brushes to apply acrylic paint to the stamps and press them directly onto the floorcloth. Tone-on-tone stamping works well for a subtle look, and mistakes aren't quite as noticeable.

6. Let each layer dry before starting on another. You may need to mask off an area, so the paint should be completely dry. If you make a mistake, you can always paint over it...but try not to.

7. When you are happy with your efforts (or just too tired to do any more) seal with several coats of sealant. You can't use too much! Walking on it with those big feet of yours is very hard on the paint, so be generous. Ten coats will keep it looking good for years and will keep you high for a few hours depending on how toxic your sealer is! But seriously folks, follow the instructions on your product of choice, and work in a well-ventilated area. Your body will thank you later.

8. You can secure the rug to the floor with a non-skid mat made for that purpose. You may even want to glue the non-skid mat to the underside of the floorcloth.

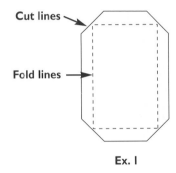

Cut lines

Fold lines

Ex. 1

Hot Potatoes stamps used: Curly Curl #N359, Tri-Curl #F357, Four Point Star #I306, Jester Border #P368, Giant Helix #J252

Wooden Mirrors

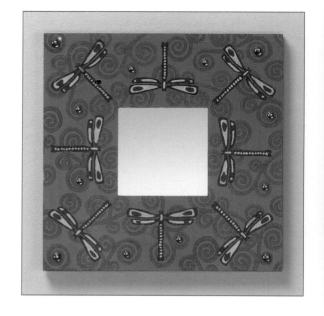

Materials - Dragonfly Mirror:

Hot Potatoes rubber stamps
Mirror with wide wooden frame
Sandpaper (if mirror frame has a finish on it)
Acrylic craft paints
Jewels
Spray sealant, such as Krylon Crystal Clear or
    polyurethane spray
Newspaper
Glue
Scissors

Steps - Dragonfly Mirror:

1. If your mirror frame has a finish on it, sand it lightly.

2. Paint the mirror frame with bright orange acrylic paint.

3. Stamp the Curly Curls in red acrylic paint. Stamp the dragonflies in purple acrylic paint.

4. Let dry and color in dragonflies and random dots with a brighter shade or metallic.
    Glue on jewels.

5. Cover mirror surface with newspaper for protection, then spray the painted mirror frame
    with sealant.

Hot Potatoes stamps used: Curly Curl #N359 and Open Dragonfly #M333

Materials - Peacock Mirror:

Hot Potatoes rubber stamps
Mirror with wide wooden frame
Sandpaper (if mirror frame has a finish on it)
Acrylic craft paints
Jewels
Spray sealant, such as Krylon Crystal Clear or
    polyurethane spray
Newspaper
Glue
Marabou
Scissors

Steps - Peacock Mirror:

1. If your mirror frame has a finish on it, sand it lightly.

2. Paint the mirror frame with turquoise acrylic paint.

3. Stamp the Peacock Feathers in dark blue, light blue, and green acrylic paint, overlapping the stamps in a random pattern.

4. Glue on jewels.

5. Cover mirror surface with newspaper for protection, then spray the painted mirror frame with sealant.

6. Cut apart one of your unused boas and glue around the edge.

Hot Potatoes stamp used: Peacock Feather #Q340

Decorative Mirror Hanger

Steps:

1. Condition the black polymer clay. The pasta machine makes it easy, but if you don't have one, cut the block of clay into pieces and begin rolling them one at a time in your hands or on your work surface until each piece is warm and pliable. Continue this procedure until you have conditioned the whole package.

2. Roll conditioned clay out into a sheet approximately 1/4" thick (or a teeny bit thicker).

3. Mist the surface of the stamps lightly with water, and then place face down onto the prepared sheet of clay. Press firmly and evenly to transfer a distinct image to the sheet of clay. The water will act as a release agent, allowing you to remove the stamp easily.

4. Use the cookie cutter or X-Acto to cut out the image in a round disc shape, smoothing the edges if necessary.

5. Using the small brush and assorted Pearl-Ex powders, color the surface of the clay to highlight the image. A little powder goes a long way! Wipe away excess.

6. Preheat the oven to 275°F. Shape the disc over a large wooden bead for a domed or curved effect. Place the disc and the bead/support onto a baking tray and bake for 30 minutes.

7. Once cool, apply 2 or more thin coats of Future floor finish before gluing on hardware to complete the ornament. I would strongly recommend a two-part epoxy for the best hold!

8. Follow the instructions on page 11 to emboss the velvet ribbon. Attach the ribbon to the back of the holder and hang. This mirror was quite heavy, so we used wire to hang the mirror from a traditional wall hanger, making the ribbon ornamental rather than functional.

Hot Potatoes stamps used: Celtic Groove Thang #L403, Tattoo You #I402

Materials:

Hot Potatoes rubber stamps
(1) package of Premo-Fimo, or other oven-fired polymer clay in black
Pasta machine (optional)
Dedicated rolling pin, or other means for rolling an even sheet of clay
Biscuit or cookie cutter to match the size of the stamped image (or an X-Acto knife and a steady hand)
Pearl-Ex powders (interference colors: red, blue, violet, green, gold)
Small soft paintbrush
Large wooden ball or bead (approximately 1-1/4" to 1-1/2" across)
Baking tray
Oven
Future floor finish
Two-part epoxy
(1) yard teal Hot Potatoes acetate/rayon velvet ribbon (3" wide)
Misting bottle with tap water
Iron (no steam)
Hardware for hanging mirror

Curtains

Steps:

1. Follow the instructions on page 11 for embossing on velvet with just one important amendment. To attach the Steam-A-Seam2 at the same time that you emboss the velvet, simply place the stamp rubber side up on the work surface and lay the velvet right side down on the stamp. Mist with water. Then lay a piece of fusible web on the wrong side of the fabric, with a layer of the protective paper on top of the webbing. Use the area of the iron without steam holes to press over the protective paper for 10 to 20 seconds. This will emboss the image of the Mum onto your velvet. The webbing will permanently bond to the velvet, making it more stable and also preventing it from fraying.

2. The curtains pictured required almost 60 velvet mum cut-outs. Cut out the mums you will need, leaving a small edge of the unembossed velvet as the border for each piece.

3. Sew a casing at the top of the curtains. Be sure it is large enough for a curtain rod to fit in easily. This particular fabric did not need to be hemmed or stitched on the sides. What a deal! They are not even hemmed at the bottom, as this net fabric does not fray. Yippee!

4. Spread out the piece of net fabric on the protected work surface. Now arrange your mums on the curtain panels. Be creative! They can be arranged in uniform rows, rows with variable spacing (horizontal or vertical), set in clusters, or scattered randomly over the surface. Steam-A-Seam2 has a tacky back so you can arrange your mums and they will stay put (to a degree) until the final ironing. After creating your pattern, carefully turn the entire piece to the wrong side. You may find it easier to work with a small area at a time. Spread the protective paper over the back of each mum and hit each one with the iron for a few seconds, securing it permanently to the tulle.

5. If you are using an ordinary fusible web, you will have to place the mums upside down to figure out the pattern, spread the fabric over the mums, then the protective paper, and iron it all. Try your best to find Steam-A-Seam2. It makes all the difference in the world.

Materials:

Hot Potatoes rubber stamp
Sheer fabric such as tulle or net (for curtain measurements you will need the length plus 10" and the width of the window times 2 1/2)
(1/2) yard pistachio acetate/rayon velvet
Thread
Sewing machine
Manicure scissors
Steam-A-Seam2 double-stick iron-on fusible web
Protective paper from the fusible web
Iron (no steam)
Misting bottle with tap water
Scissors

Hot Potatoes stamp used: Mum #L405

Bird Mobile

Materials:

Hot Potatoes rubber stamps
Small scraps of acetate/rayon velvet (approximately
  7" x 5") in burgundy, red, teal, pistachio, and cobalt
Ball of colorful yarn
Embroidery thread in colors to contrast
  with velvet
Needle
(3) yards of ribbon
(5) decorative beads
(10) seed beads for eyes
Gold tassel
Iron (no steam)
Misting bottle with tap water
Poly-fil stuffing
Scissors
Pins
Tracing paper

Steps:

1. Copy pattern on page 116, and cut 2 birds from each of the 5 colors of velvet.

2. Follow the instructions on page 11 to emboss the birds.

3. Pin the birds, wrong sides together. Hand stitch on right side, using a decorative blanket stitch (see diagram below). Leave an opening at the top and bottom of each bird to stuff and run the ribbon through.

4. Stuff each bird generously with the Poly-fil.

5. Loop the ribbon in half. Make a knot 3" from the folded end.

6. Run this through the openings in the first bird and slipstitch the opening to close.

7. Sew up both openings in the bird.

8. Run the ribbon through a bead, leaving about 1" on either side. Repeat until all the birds and beads are on the mobile.

9. Tie 1 more knot in the ribbon and attach the last bead. Sew on the tassel and cover the sewing by sliding the last bead down over it.

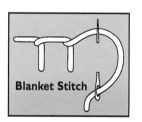

Blanket Stitch

10. Sew seed beads on the birds where the eyes should be.

11. Make tassels out of the colorful yarn by looping four or five lengths of yarn. Tie or knot the tassels and sew these to the tail of each bird.

This is one of my favorite projects. I also cut patterns such as irregular shaped stars and hearts from newspaper and used them to make more mobiles. Use your imagination. The possibilities are endless!

Hot Potatoes stamps used:
Mum #L405, Curly Curl #N359, Open Daisy #L423, Celtic Groove Thang #L403, Giant Helix #J252

Beaded Velvet Lampshade

These truly add a bordello look in your boudoir, but have a little fun and take a walk on the wild side.

Materials:

Hot Potatoes rubber stamp
(1/3) yard burgundy acetate/rayon velvet
(1) package of Steam-A-Seam2 double-stick
   iron-on fusible web
Protective paper from the fusible web
Iron (no steam)
Misting bottle with tap water
Manicure scissors
Self-adhesive lampshade
Fabric or white glue
Beaded trim for bottom edge of shade (you can
   bead it yourself, but why?)

Steps:

1. Follow the instructions for Velvet Embossing™ on page 11 with one amendment. You will attach the fusible web at the same time that you emboss the velvet. Simply place the stamp rubber side up on your work surface and lay the velvet right side down on the stamp. Mist with water. Then lay a piece of fusible web on the wrong side of the fabric and a layer of the protective paper on top of the web. Using the area of the iron without steam holes, press the protective paper for 10 to 20 seconds. This will emboss the image of the leaf onto your velvet. The fusible web will permanently bond to the velvet, making it more stable and also preventing it from fraying.

2. Emboss about 20 of the Tahitian Leaf images on the burgundy velvet. Try to emboss them close together to save that pricey velvet. Use the manicure scissors to cut out all the leaves leaving a small edge of the unembossed velvet as the border for each leaf.

3. Glue the trim along the bottom edge of the lampshade. Working on the lampshade is easiest if the shade is actually sitting on the lamp.

4. Try to find a lampshade with a self-stick surface. The project is so much easier with that one element. Simply apply the leaves to the shade starting with the bottom row and working up to the top. Turn the light on from time to time to make sure there are no big gaps where the light shines through.

5. After you are satisfied with the placement of the leaves, use the glue to permanently attach them to the shade. Just a dot or two on each leaf will suffice.

Hot Potatoes stamp used: #1248 Tahitian Leaf

Woven Ribbon Photo Transfer Pillows

Materials:

For Either Pillow:

Hot Potatoes rubber stamps
Iron-on photo transfer paper
Photograph
Poly-fil stuffing or pillow form
Scissors
Iron (no steam)
Misting bottle with tap water
Needle
Thread
Sewing machine

Flamingo Ribbon Transfer Pillow:

(1) yard teal Hot Potatoes acetate/rayon
   velvet ribbon (2" wide)
(1) yard pistachio Hot Potatoes
   acetate/rayon velvet ribbon (2' wide)
(2) yards cobalt blue Hot Potatoes
   acetate/rayon velvet ribbon (2' wide)
(1) 7" x 7" piece of cream muslin or cotton
(1) 15" x 15" piece of cream muslin or cotton
(1) 15" x 15" piece of Steam-A-Seam2
   double-stick iron-on fusible web
Protective paper from the fusible web
(1) 15" x 15" piece of fabric for back of pillow

Sisters Ribbon Transfer Pillow:

(1) yard pistachio Hot Potatoes
   acetate/rayon velvet ribbon (2' wide)
(2) yards burgundy Hot Potatoes
   acetate/rayon velvet ribbon (2' wide)
(1) yard each of 2 different ribbon trims
(1) 4" x 6" piece of cream muslin or cotton
(1) 12" x 12" piece of cream muslin or cotton
(1) 12" x 12" piece of Steam-A-Seam2
   double-stick iron-on fusible web
Protective paper from the fusible web
(1) 12" x 12" piece of fabric for back of pillow

Steps:

1. Follow the instructions on page 11 to emboss the velvet ribbon.

2. Scan the photo to the size you want and print it out on photo transfer paper, or take the photo to a copy center to have it scanned and printed. Following the directions on the photo transfer paper, transfer the image to a piece of cream muslin or cotton, centering it on the fabric.

3. Lay the Steam-A-Seam2 fusible web on a flat surface with the adhesive side up. Remove the paper covering from the fusible web and set it aside for later use. Lay the photo and embossed ribbon on the fusible interfacing (with right sides up). Because the Steam-A-Seam2 is sticky, it holds everything in place while you design your ribbon pattern.

4. Carefully turn over the entire project. Using the paper from the fusible web to cover and protect the ribbon and an iron set to medium, gently iron the ribbon and photo to the fusible web from the back side.

5. Remove the paper backing from the fusible web and lay the 15" x 15" square of muslin on top of it. With the iron set to medium gently iron the muslin backing to the pillow front. If these pillows are going to be used for more than just decorative purposes, you may want to go ahead and reinforce the ribbon by sewing it (along the edges) to the backing.

6. With right sides together, sew the pillow back to the pillow front around all four sides, leaving a 3" opening. Turn the pillow right side out.

7. Stuff the pillow with Poly-fil stuffing or insert a pillow form. Slipstitch the opening to finish.

Hot Potatoes stamps used:
Flamingo Pillow: Leaf Trio #L394 and Small Dots #J420 – Sisters Pillow: Tattoo You #I402

Woven Ribbon Pillow

Steps:

1. Follow the instructions on page 11 to emboss all of the velvet ribbon.

2. Lay the Steam-A-Seam2 fusible web on a flat surface with the adhesive side up. Remove the paper covering from the fusible web and set it aside for later use. Lay out the embossed ribbon on the fusible web with right sides up. Because the Steam-A-Seam2 is sticky, it holds everything in place while you design your ribbon pattern. Weave the pattern as shown.

Materials:

Hot Potatoes rubber stamps
(1) yard red Hot Potatoes acetate/rayon velvet ribbon (4" wide)
(1) yard cobalt blue Hot Potatoes acetate/rayon velvet ribbon (2" wide)
(1) yard cobalt blue Hot Potatoes acetate/rayon velvet ribbon (3" wide)
(1) yard green Hot Potatoes acetate/rayon velvet ribbon (2" wide)
(1) yard green Hot Potatoes acetate/rayon velvet ribbon (3" wide)
(1) 14" x 14" piece of cream muslin or cotton
(1) 14" x 14" piece of Steam-A-Seam2 double-stick iron-on fusible web
Protective paper from the fusible web
(1) 14" x 14" piece of fabric for back of pillow
Poly-fil stuffing or pillow form
Scissors
Iron (no steam)
Misting bottle with tap water
Needle
Thread
Sewing machine

3. Carefully turn over the entire piece. Using the paper from the fusible web to cover and protect the ribbon and an iron set on medium, gently iron the ribbon to the fusible web from the back side.

4. Remove the paper backing from the fusible web and lay the 14" x 14" square of muslin on top of it. With the iron set to medium, gently iron the muslin backing to the pillow front. If these pillows are going to be used for more than just decorative purposes, you may want to go ahead and reinforce the ribbon by sewing it (along the edges) to the backing.

5. With right sides together, sew the pillow back to the pillow front around all four sides, leaving a 3" opening. Turn the pillow right side out.

6. Stuff the pillow with Poly-fil stuffing or insert a pillow form. Slipstitch the opening to finish.

Hot Potatoes stamps used:
Puff #Q395, Asian Coin #E396, Hari Kari #F401, Discovery #J345

Velvet Ribbon Picture Frame Matting

Materials:

Hot Potatoes rubber stamp
(1-1/2) yards pistachio Hot Potatoes
   acetate/rayon velvet ribbon (3" wide)
9" x 12" picture frame with white
   mat board cut to fit picture and frame
Fabric adhesive or Red Line
   double-stick tape
Foam tape
Scissors
Iron (no steam)
Misting bottle with tap water

Steps:

1. Follow the instructions on page 11 to emboss the velvet ribbon.

2. With adhesive or Red Line double-stick tape, attach the velvet ribbon to the top and the bottom of the mat board. Position the ribbon so that 1/4" of the inside edge of the mat board shows. Then attach the ribbon to the sides of the mat board, again leaving the 1/4" edge of the mat board showing.

3. Trim any excess ribbon off the outside edges of the mat board.

4. Place a piece of foam tape in each corner of the piece to be framed to create space so that the glass does not crush the velvet.

5. Assemble the frame as usual.

Hot Potatoes stamp used: Curly Leaf #1393

Wine Crate Footstools

Materials:

Basic footstool materials:
Hot Potatoes rubber stamps
Wooden wine crate
1/2" plywood piece cut to the exact measurement
   of the top of the box
Batting
Foam piece cut to the same dimensions as your
   plywood top piece
Wood glue
Foam paintbrushes
Household paintbrush
Sandpaper
Staple gun
Spackle
Putty knife
Scissors

Prep work for either box:

1. The first thing you have to do is go to the liquor store and nab a couple of wooden wine crates. These cost around $6.00 each. That's fair.

2. Prep the box for painting by using spackle to cover up any logos or knotholes. Smooth the spackle with the putty knife and let it dry.

3. Sand the spackled areas. Repeat if necessary.

Cont. on page 86

Velvet Covered Stool

Materials:

Basic stool materials (see page 85)

Latex paint in dark umber or any other very dark color except black

(3) coordinating colors of latex paint (I used cobalt blue, lime green, and turquoise)

(5) yards of decorative trim (used to mask work under the top of the stool)

Pistachio acetate/rayon velvet large enough to extend 10" beyond the plywood top (if your plywood is
14" x 20", the fabric needs to be large enough to extend 10" each way beyond the box lid)

(4) drawer pulls or cabinet knobs. The best ones are knobs that have separate screws.

(3) stencil brushes

Steps:

1. Paint the spackled and sanded box and plywood piece with dark umber paint. Let dry.

2. Plan the design with the tile stamps so that your design will fit properly on the sides of the wine crate. Allow about 1/4" between "tile" stampings to show for the "grout."

3. Use three colors on the tiles for a more textured and realistic look. First paint the tile stamp with one color. Using a stencil brush, stipple the second and third colors in a haphazard fashion. To stipple means to put the stencil brush in your paint color and apply with a straight up and down movement. You only want some of the second and third colors to show.

4. Now stamp the tile design on to the sides of the wine crate. Start in the center and work your way out.

5. Attach the 4 drawer pulls or knobs to the bottom of the box by screwing them into the wood.

6. Glue decorative trim along the unfinished top edge of the wine crate.

7. Next, emboss the velvet using the Velvet Embossing™ instructions on page 11.

8. Place the foam on top of the piece of plywood. Put several layers of batting on top of the foam. Stretch the velvet over the batting and secure it with the staple gun to the underside of the plywood in the same way you might stretch a canvas.

9. Trim the excess velvet. Cover the edge of the velvet and exposed staples by gluing on the decorative braid.

Hot Potatoes stamps used: Mum #L405, Tile Stamp Kit

Striped Stool

Steps:

1. Tape off stripes with masking tape.

2. Before painting the stripes, water down the fabric paint (or whatever paint you use). A ratio of 1 part paint and 1 part water works well. Shallow lines cut with a razor along the edge of the masking tape will keep the paints from bleeding. Paint the stripes around the entire box with a foam brush and wipe off excess paint for a color-washed look.

3. Paint the wooden knobs and glue or screw them onto the box at the bottom corners.

4. Glue decorative trim along the unfinished top edge of the wine crate.

5. Use the dark periwinkle paint to stamp the daisies onto the white cotton fabric. Allow the daisies to dry.

6. Iron Steam-A-Seam2 double-stick fusible web to the back of the daisy-printed fabric and to the smaller piece of the bright fabric you selected for the cover. Cut out the thirteen daisies. Cut out thirteen dots of the cover fabric for the center of the daisies.

7. Place the daisies and the dots on the cover fabric in a pleasing design. The fusible web has a sticky back and will hold the daisies and dots in place while you plan your design..

8. Apply the Therm O Web vinyl to the top of the cover fabric, following the instructions on the packaging.

9. Place the foam on top of the piece of plywood. Put several layers of batting on top of the foam. Stretch the fabric over the batting and secure it with the staple gun to the under side of the plywood in the same way you might stretch a canvas.

10. Trim the excess fabric. Cover the edge of the fabric and staples by gluing on decorative braid.

Materials:

Basic stool materials (see page 85)

Acrylic craft paint in desired colors (or any other waterbased paint you might have – I have even used Jacquard fabric paints)

(4) drawer pulls or cabinet knobs. The best ones are knobs that have separate screws.

(5) yards of decorative trim (used to mask work under the top of the stool)

Bright fabric for the stool top large enough to extend 10" beyond plywood on all sides (if your plywood is 14" x 20", the fabric needs to be large enough to extend 10" each way beyond the box lid)

Another small piece of the same fabric for the dots in the center of the daisies

Piece of white cotton fabric, large enough to print 13 daisies on

Steam-a-Seam2 double-stick iron-on fusible web

Therm O Web iron-on vinyl

Scissors

Masking tape

Single edge razor blade or X-acto

Hot Potatoes stamp used: Daisy #1309

Jacquard fabric paints used: Goldenrod #JAC102, Ruby Red #JAC107, Emerald Green #JAC117, Dark Periwinkle #JAC125, Turquoise #JAC114

Three-Piece Desk Set

Materials:

Hot Potatoes rubber stamp
Cobalt blue acetate/rayon velvet (about 1/2 yard covers all 3 pieces)
Glue or Red Line double-stick tape
Spray adhesive
Scissors
Iron (no steam)
Misting bottle with tap water

If your desk looked any better you wouldn't get any work done!

PENCIL CUP

Additional Materials:

Metal can (washed) from canned vegetables, fruit, or juice

Steps:

1. Cut a strip of paper the height of the can and wrap it around the can to determine circumference. Cut the velvet 2" longer and 2" taller than the paper pattern. Emboss the velvet according to the instructions on page 11.

2. Fold one edge of the velvet down and use glue or Red Line tape to attach it to the can. Wrap the velvet around the can keeping it tight. When you have wrapped the velvet all the way around, cover the starting point of the velvet by folding the remaining edge under and using glue or Red Line tape to attach it to the can

4. Cut slits in the excess velvet around the top and bottom of the can. Tuck the top pieces inside the cup, gluing as you go. Repeat for the bottom, gluing the bottom pieces to the bottom of the can.

5. For a more finished look, line the can with decorative paper.

LETTER HOLDER

Additional Materials:

Black heavy cardboard
Cardstock
Scotch tape
X-acto knife for cutting cardboard

Steps:

1. Enlarge the pattern on page 116 to the size you desire. Enlarge both pieces exactly the same percentage.

2. Lay pattern piece #1 onto your black cardboard and cut out. Score the lines to be folded.

3. Lay the larger pattern piece #2 that will be covered in velvet onto the cardstock and cut out. Score the 2 lines to be folded.

4. Cut and emboss enough velvet to cover the bigger piece, adding about a 1" allowance around each edge. (See page 11 for Velvet Embossing™ instructions.)

5. Assemble piece #1, folding up sides and taping into place. Tape on the inside so you do not have any tape showing on the outside of the box. The front and back will be covered, and no one will ever see the inside of the box.

6. Cover piece #2 of cardstock with the Embossed Velvet™, attaching the velvet with spray adhesive. Glue the edges as they wrap to the backside. Cut slits at the corners and peaks to make covering easier. (See example on page 69.)

7. Fold the covered piece along the 2 score lines. (See drawing at right.) Align and glue this covered piece to the black box, starting at the base. Secure the front and the back with glue or Red Line tape.

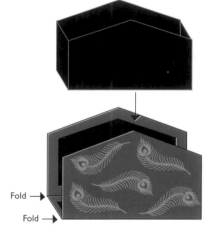

Fold →
Fold →

Hot Potatoes stamp used: Peacock Feather #Q340

BLOTTER

Additional Materials:

(1) 12" x 18" piece of white mat board
(2) 12" x 12" pieces of mat board
Red Line double-stick tape
Batting or thin foam for side pieces

Steps:

1. Lay out all 3 pieces of mat board so that the 2 small pieces are flush on either side of the large piece.

2. Tape the 2 end pieces to the larger board on one side only. Flip both pieces over on top of the larger board.

3. Cut batting or foam to fit each side piece and glue down.

4. Cut 2 pieces of velvet 14 " x 4" and emboss. (See page 11 for Velvet Embossing™ instructions.)

5. Fold the 2 side pieces back from the large piece and turn the entire piece over.

6. Cover the 2 side pieces with the Embossed Velvet™ by gluing excess edges under the outermost edges only.

7. Turn the whole piece over again and flip the covered side pieces back up. Finish by gluing under the excess edges, pulling tightly as you go.

NOTE: This blotter is made to accommodate an 11' x 17' calendar.

Hot Potatoes stamp used: Peacock Feather #Q340

Faux Tile Cigar Box/Bug Collection

Materials - Faux Tile Cigar Box:

Hot Potatoes Tile Stamp Kit (contains 5 foam stamps) or
   cut stamps from E-Z Cut
(3) coordinating colors of acrylic paint
Acrylic paint in dark brown or gray
(3) stencil brushes
(3) foam paintbrushes
Spray polyurethane
Wooden cigar box
Spackle
Sandpaper

The only reason my husband smokes cigars is so that he can supply me with the boxes for this project. He's so nice. Smelly but nice.

Steps - Faux Tile Cigar Box:

1. Use spackle to cover any logos or rough spots that may be in the cigar box. Allow the putty to dry and sand smooth. Repeat if necessary.

2. Paint your box with a base coat of dark brown or gray. This color will represent your "grout." Work from the center cut.

3. Plan your design with the tile stamps so that the design will fit properly in the area you are working on. Always allow about 1/4" between "tile" stampings to show the "grout."

4. Use 3 colors on the tiles for a more textured and realistic look. First, use a foam paintbrush to cover the surface of the tile stamp with one color. Using a stencil brush, stipple the second and third colors onto the surface of the stamp in a random fashion, by putting the stencil brush in your paint and applying it with a straight up and down movement. The second and third colors are accent colors, so they should not completely cover the stamp. This technique is simple, but a small amount of practice is advised.

5. Use the foam tile stamp to imprint the box. Always start in the center and work your way out. Try to use different sizes of stamps. This gives the finished piece a more realistic look.

6. After the entire project is completed, allow the paint to dry. Spray the entire surface with polyurethane to make the "tile" really pop!

NOTE: Don't scrutinize each time you stamp. The imperfections in this technique are what makes the tiles work.

Cont. on page 94

BUG COLLECTION

Materials:

Hot Potatoes rubber stamps
Wooden cigar box
Teal acetate/rayon velvet large enough to cover the
    top and bottom of your cigar box
(2) pieces of cardboard to fit inside the top and
    bottom of the cigar box
White cardstock
Marvy Markers
Glue
Glitter
Straight pins
Red Line double-stick tape
Scissors
Iron (no steam)
Misting bottle with tap water
X-acto for cutting cardboard

Steps:

1. Cut the cardboard to fit inside the bottom and the top of the box. These pieces should be about an 1/8" smaller than the area they fit in, as they will be covered with velvet.

2. Cut a piece of velvet to cover each of the cardboard pieces, adding an extra inch on all sides for overlap.

3. Follow the Velvet Embossing™ instructions on page 11 to emboss the 2 pieces of velvet with the Curly Leaf stamp.

4. Cover the cardboard and secure inside the cigar box with the Red Line tape.

5. Color different parts of the bugs with Marvy Markers in bright colors and then stamp the bugs on the cardstock. Stamp 2 imprints of each bug you want in your collection.

6. Cut out the bugs.

7. Apply a thin coat of glue to each bug and sprinkle liberally with glitter. Allow to dry.

8. Take two identical bugs and glue them together at the head and body only. Use your fingers to bend the wings up slightly for a 3-D effect.

9. Use straight pins to tack the bugs into the box.

10. Scare your friends who have some unreasonable fear of bugs (especially bugs covered in glitter).

Hot Potatoes stamps used:
Curly Leaf #1393, Skeeter #L406, Japanese Beetle #L407 (You can, of course, increase your collection.)

Bug Wall Hanging

Materials:

Hot Potatoes rubber stamps
(6) 4" x 2-3/8" manila tags
Brown or other earth-tone mulberry paper, torn to measure
   approximately 4" x 18"
Self-stick wall hanger
PVA or archival glue
Marvy Markers in lots of colors
Ruler
Sponge

Steps:

1. Color the bug stamps with markers, then stamp. This allows you to get different colors for different bug body parts.

2. Stamp all the tags with a combination of bugs and the various leaf stamps. Then use markers to add details on the bugs as shown in the photograph.

3. Tear the mulberry paper to the desired size (approximately 4" x 18").

4. Use PVA or archival glue to attach the tags to the mulberry paper.

5. Place a self-stick hanger on the back of the mulberry paper so you can hang the artwork on the wall.

TIP: To get the rough deckled edge on the mulberry paper, score the edge of the paper with the edge of a ruler and moisten with a sponge on both sides. Tear carefully to create the look of handmade paper.

Hot Potatoes stamps used:
Cicada #I419, Skeeter #L406, Japanese Beetle #L407, Leaf Trio #L394, Feather Leaf #J392

Make several of these at a time. A pack of 3 makes a nice presentation.

Notable Notebooks with Batik Covers

Materials:

Hot Potatoes rubber stamp
Notepads made from legal pads – several sizes
are available at your local office supply store
Cardstock the same size as the front of the
notepad you want to cover
White mulberry paper
Misting bottle with tap water
Dye-based inks (3 colors of Dr. Martins
watercolor inks were used in this presentation)
Clear resist inkpad
Box top or tray to work in
Iron
Plain newsprint
Red Line double-stick tape, or bookbinders glue
(Yes glue is a good brand)
Decorative yarns, ribbons, or threads
for embellishment
Coordinating cardstock for trim
Scissors
Clear embossing powder
Embossing gun

Steps:

1. Stamp the dragonfly onto the mulberry paper using the clear resist inkpad.

2. Emboss the images with clear embossing powder, following the manufacturer's instructions.

3. Place the paper in the box top or tray and use the misting bottle to wet it generously.

4. Dilute the watercolor inks and use the drop applicators to drop colors onto the wet paper. You can use fingers, brushes, or other tools to help the colors mix and blend.

5. Hang the paper to dry or use a hair dryer to speed the process. Do not use a heat gun!

6. Iron the paper between two sheets of unprinted newsprint. The heat from the iron will cause the embossing powder to melt into the newsprint.

7. Cut a piece of the decorated mulberry paper the same size as the cover of your notepad and also a piece of cardstock the same size.

8. Cut a strip of coordinating cardstock about 2" long that measures the width of the notepad.

9. Use the Red Line double-stick tape or bookbinders glue to attach the batik paper you have created to the cover cardstock. Position this over the front of the notebook and secure with Red Line tape.

10. Run a strip of Red Line tape across the top edge of the notebook, front and back, and secure decorative ribbon.

11. Run Red Line tape along all edges of the coordinating piece of cardstock. Position across the top front of the notebook.

12. Tie the ribbon, yarn, or threads, and fold the cardstock over the top to hide seams and ribbon attachments.

Hot Potatoes stamp used: Curly Leaf #I393, Skeeter #L406, Black Dragonfly #J332

Great for parties. Stack the deck to suit your guest list!

Fortune Telling Cards

Materials:

Hot Potatoes rubber stamps
Water-based inkpads
(2) Hot Potatoes Dragonfly/Bamboo Resist Paper
  Accordion Cards
Glue or Red Line double-stick tape
(7) 4" x 2-3/8" manila tags, available at your
  local office supply store
(7) 2" x 4" coin envelopes, available at your
  local office supply store

Steps:

1. Color the panels of 2 accordion resist cards. Make each panel a different color. This card was done with Ranger Dye Pads. You can use makeup sponges to pick up the color from your inkpad and then apply the color to the paper. Continue to apply color until you have an even, smooth coat of color. It helps to mask off any panels you do not wish to color to keep them clean. Repeat until all panels are colored.

2. Extend the accordion by using glue or Red Line double-stick tape to attach the last panel of one card over the first panel of the next card.

3. Stamp a letter on each coin envelope to form the word DESTINY. Use a variety of Asian images and randomly stamp the coin envelopes.

4. Stamp the tags with various images. On the back of the tags write humorous fortunes, or glue on fortunes that you have retrieved from a batch of fortune cookies or downloaded from Internet sites.

NOTE: The "FATE" card is done the same way except only one accordion card is used. It is the Wildflower/Fern pattern. Colors were applied with makeup sponges and blended.

Hot Potatoes stamps used:
Uppercase Alphabet Kit #HPUC2, Dragonfly #G039, Ginkgo #K339, Prosperity #I399, Energy #G400, Asian
Coin #E396, Baby Light My Fire #I381, Yoko-Mono #W384

Snail Mail Hanging Card

Materials:

Hot Potatoes rubber stamps
(4) 8" x 4" pieces of burnt orange cardstock
(4) 7" x 3" pieces of off-white cardstock
Black marker
Standard business size envelope
(55") of black ribbon (1" wide)
Assorted water-based inkpads
  and Marvy Markers
Glitter glue
Glue, glue stick, or spray adhesive
Scotch tape
Post-it Notes
Paper towel
Scissors

Steps:

1. Use the Escargot to stamp onto a Post-it Note. Make sure that part of the image extends into the area with adhesive on the back. Cut out around the outside of the Escargot image to make a mask.

2. Ink the alphabet stamps to print out the words you need on each piece of cardstock. On the first one, stamp the S, the E, and then place the Escargot mask down before stamping the letter N. With the mask in place stamp the letter N. Leave the Escargot in place and finally stamp the letter D. Do this for each piece of off-white cardstock until all 4 words of your message are spelled out, placing the Escargot in a different spot on each card. Use the Escargot stamp to fill space left by your mask.

3. Use a variety of stamps and colorful inkpads or markers to randomly stamp the remaining blank space on the cards.

4. Use the glitter glue to cover each Escargot. He needs all the personality he can get!

5. Stamp the envelope. Wad up the paper towel. Tap it onto an inkpad and use it as a stamp to create a subtle background and fill in all white space. Use the Escargot stamp and cover him with glitter again.

6. Glue each decorated piece of cardstock onto the burnt orange paper.

7. Draw a fine line around each piece of decorated cardstock with the black marker.

8. Turn all 3 layered cards upside down. Line them up as you want them to hang, with about 1" between each card

9. Fold the black ribbon in half and position to allow a loop above the first card for hanging. Lay the ribbon so that it runs evenly behind all the cards and secure with Scotch tape.

10. Glue the final card into the envelope.

TIP: You will probably only find white business envelopes. If you stamp up the envelope heavily and fill in the background (see step 5), no one will ever know the envelope was white.

Hot Potatoes stamps used:
Uppercase Alphabet Kit #HPUC2, Escargot #G331, Leaf Trio #L394, Mum #L405, Small Open Fern #J249, Giant Helix #J252

Kimono Hanging Card

Steps:

1. Cut the Wildflower/Fern resist card into separate panels on the prefolded lines. Use separate sponges to absorb color from the inkpads to dab on each card. Saturate the cards with color for a strong result. Working with the red first, color the entire card and then softly blend the darker shade of red around the edges. Repeat on another card with green, and on the third with blue. Wipe off excess ink with paper towels and the preprinted resist design will show through.

2. Cut the Dragonfly/Bamboo card into separate panels on the prescored lines. Repeat the coloring process from step 1 and sponge color on 3 different panels. Wipe any excess ink off the card. Allow to dry for 3 minutes.

3. Ink the kimono stamps with permanent black ink and stamp over each of the Dragonfly/Bamboo cards from step 2.

4. After the black ink dries, cut out each kimono. Mount each kimono on a panel of the first cards you made in step 1. Glue in place.

5. Outline the edge of each rectangular card with the gold paint pen.

6. Glue these decorated cards to the black cardstock. Outline the edge of each black card with the gold paint pen.

7. Turn all 3 layered cards upside down. Line them up as you want them to hang, with about 1" between each card.

8. Fold the black ribbon in half and position to allow a loop above the first card for hanging. Lay the ribbon so that it runs evenly behind all the cards and secure with Scotch tape.

TIP: Resist paper takes longer to dry than some, so be careful not to smear the ink. If you mess up a panel, do not throw the card out. Instead, cut it up and use the decorative part for layering or collage.

Materials:

Hot Potatoes rubber stamps
(1) Hot Potatoes Dragonfly/Bamboo Resist Paper Accordion Card
(1) Hot Potatoes Wildflower/Fern Resist Paper Accordion Card
(3) pieces of black cardstock (8" square)
Dye-based inkpads: (2) shades of red, (2) shades of green, (2) shades of blue, and (1) gold
(8) cosmetic sponges
Glue, glue stick, or spray adhesive
Gold paint pen
Paper towels
Permanent black inkpad
(65") black grosgrain ribbon (1" wide)
Scotch tape
Scissors

Sailboat Hanging Card

Steps:

1. Use the Lighthouse, Sailboat, and Venus Shell stamps to imprint images onto the white cardstock with the white pigment ink. One image will be on each piece of white cardstock.

2. Emboss with the clear embossing powder (see page 18) and allow to cool completely.

3. Using a separate sponge for each color, apply the purple, blue, and green ink to the three pieces of white cardstock. Dab sponges on the inkpads and then dab the colors onto the cards. Blend the 3 colors together as shown in the photograph. The color goes over the embossed images, and then you immediately rub it off.

4. Lightly mist all 3 cards that you have just decorated. Allow to dry completely (approximately 20 minutes).

5. Apply glue to the back of the 3 pieces of marbled paper and cover the 5" pieces of cardstock.

6. Apply glue to the back of 3 pieces of purple cardstock and mount them onto the center of each marbled card. Repeat this with the 3 decorated pieces of cardstock.

7. Turn all 3 layered cards upside down. Line them up as you want them to hang, with about 1" between each card.

8. Fold the purple ribbon in half and position to allow a loop above the first card for hanging. Lay the ribbon so that it runs evenly behind all the cards and secure with Scotch tape.

Materials:

Hot Potatoes rubber stamps
(3) pieces of cardstock (5" square)
(3) pieces of glossy purple cardstock (4" square)
(3) pieces of plain white paper cardstock (3" square)
(3) pieces of marbled paper (7" square)
White pigment inkpad
Clear embossing powder
Embossing gun
Water-based inkpads in green, blue, and purple
Misting bottle with tap water
Glue, glue stick, or spray adhesive
(3) cosmetic sponges
(45") piece of purple ribbon (1" wide)
Scotch tape
Scissors

Hot Potatoes stamps used: Lighthouse #L374, Sailboat #N373, Venus Shell #O371

Shadowbox Hanging Card

Steps:

1. Use the purple ink to stamp El Sol, Star Cup and Whirlybird, one per card, on each of the 3 pieces of white cardstock.

2. Emboss with the clear embossing powder (see page 18) and allow to dry until it is cool to touch.

3. Use the cosmetic sponges to apply the water-based colors to cards. Start with the yellow in the center, then the orange, and finally the pink. Blend softly.

4. Layer each decorated piece onto a piece of the purple cardstock and glue.

5. Wrap the red paper around each box lid as you might cover a gift box.

6. Glue a piece of gold cardstock inside each box lid.

7. Take 1 of the 2" x 7" strips of gold paper and fold it into a rectangular shape (see Example 1). These are going to create the 3-D mounts behind each decorated card.

8. Tape the ends together and glue the long side to the back of the decorated card. Glue or tape the other long side into the box. Repeat with the remaining 2 pieces of gold paper.

9. Turn all 3 layered shadowboxes upside down. Line them up as you want them to hang, with about 1" between each card.

10. Fold the red ribbon in half and position to allow a loop above the first card for hanging. Lay the ribbon so that it runs evenly behind all the cards and secure with Scotch tape.

Materials:

Hot Potatoes rubber stamps
(3) lids from gift boxes (bracelet size, approximately 5" square)
(3) pieces of gold cardstock to fit inside each lid
(3) 2" x 7" pieces of gold cardstock
(3) pieces of red paper to cover each box lid (7-1/2" square)
(3) pieces of purple cardstock (3" square)
(3) pieces of white cardstock (3" square)
Purple pigment inkpad
Clear embossing ink
Embossing gun
Water-based inkpads in pink, orange, and yellow
(3) cosmetic sponges
(45") piece of red ribbon (1" wide)
Scotch tape
Glue, glue stick, or spray adhesive
Scissors

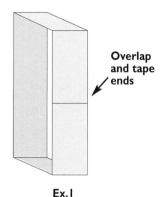

Overlap and tape ends

Ex. 1

Hot Potatoes stamps used: El Sol #J251, Star Cup #1178, Whirlybird #N070

Holiday Stockings

Hot Potatoes rubber stamps
(1/3) yard of teal acetate/rayon velvet
(16") of red Hot Potatoes acetate/rayon
   velvet ribbon (2" wide)
(16") of cobalt blue Hot Potatoes acetate/rayon
   velvet ribbon (2" wide)
Matching thread
Needle
Sewing machine
Scissors
(10") of gold fringe
(12") of gold braid for hanger
Res-Q Tape
Iron (no steam)
Misting bottle with tap water
Tracing paper

Steps:

1. Enlarge the pattern on page 116 until the top edge of the stocking is 8" across. This is easily done on a copy machine. Use the pattern to cut 2 stocking pieces out of the teal velvet.

2. Emboss the velvet, following the instructions on page 11.

3. With right sides together sew these 2 pieces together, leaving the top open (seam allowance 1/2"). Turn right side out. Clip curves and trim seam allowance.

4. Emboss the 2 pieces of velvet ribbon (see page 11) with the Small Dots stamp.

5. Remove the wire from the ribbon. Sew the 2 pieces of ribbon together by overlapping the red piece slightly over the cobalt piece. This will be the stocking cuff.

6. Machine or hand sew the gold trim along the bottom edge of the red ribbon.

7. Fold the ribbon cuff in half, with right sides together and stitch, leaving a 1/2" seam allowance. Turn right side out.

8. Slip the cuff inside the stocking with the right side of the cuff against the wrong side of the stocking. Stitch along the top of the stocking.

9. Trim seam allowance and turn cuff over the top of the stocking.

10. Make a loop of gold braid for the hanger and tie a knot or bow at the end. Tack the loop onto the stocking with needle and thread.

NOTE: The other 2 stockings are made the same way except they are 6" across at the top edge of the cuff. Ribbon 4" wide is used to make the cuffs in a single piece. (See step 8 above.) For the red or cobalt stocking you need 1/4 yard of velvet and 14" lengths of ribbon.

Hot Potatoes stamps used:
Teal Stocking: Olive Dots #P421, Small Dots #J420
Red Stocking: Big Dots #U422, Olive Dots #P421
Cobalt Blue Stocking: Tri-Curl #F357, Jack #F310

Tabletop Christmas Tree Skirt

Materials:

Hot Potatoes rubber stamps
(1/3) yard of red acetate/rayon velvet
(1/3) yard of contrasting fabric for lining
Res-Q Tape
Thread to match
(5) yards of gold fringe
(3) gold buttons
(5) gold jingle bells
(5) yards of red Hot Potatoes
    acetate/rayon velvet ribbon (2" wide)
Iron (no steam)
Misting bottle with tap water
Sewing machine
Velcro
Needle
Scissors
String
Tailor's chalk

Steps:

1. Cut a 12" square from the red velvet. Fold the velvet in half, and then in half again.

2. Holding a string at center point, attach tailor's chalk and mark a cutting line for the round skirt. Make this circle as full as possible.

3. Cut a small circle cut of the center point where the fabric folds come together. (See diagram at right.)

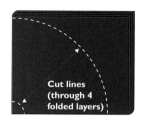

Cut lines
(through 4
folded layers)

4. Unfold the velvet and cut a straight line along one of the folds from the center hole to the edge of the velvet skirt.

5. Repeat all of the above for the lining.

6. Following the instructions on page 11, emboss the tree skirt in a random pattern.

7. Use Res-Q Tape instead of basting to put the skirt and lining together, right sides facing. The Res-Q Tape should be in the seam allowance.

8. Stitch all edges together, leaving an 8" opening on one of the straight sides. Do not sew through the Res-Q tape as it leaves the needle sticky. Trim the edges and clip the curves.

9. Remove the Res-Q Tape. Turn right side out. Machine stitch the opening closed.

10. Stitch the gold fringe around the edge of the skirt.

11. Sew the 3 buttons on. Omit buttonholes and attach Velcro to hold the skirt together.

12. Emboss the 5 yards of ribbon and cut into 5 equal pieces, 1 yard long.

13. Fold one end of each piece to make a point and sew one bell on each point, tacking the point together at the same time.

14. Carefully pull an inch or so of wire from the unfinished edge of each piece. Use this wire to secure velvet trim to treetop.

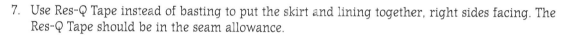

NOTE: To make a full-size tree skirt, you will need a full yard of velvet for a 36" square, a full yard of lining, 5 buttons and 3 yards of fringe. The amount of ribbon trim for the tree will depend on the height of your tree.

Hot Potatoes stamps used: Snowflake Dos #O316, Snowflake Three #G084

Holiday Garlands

Materials:

Hot Potatoes rubber stamps
Foam Core
Thick cardboard to protect your cutting surface
Dye-based inkpads and/or markers in desired colors
X-Acto knife with extra blades
Yarn, embroidery thread, or green dental floss
Embroidery needle
Glue
Scissors

Steps:

1. Color the stamps with either markers or stamp pads. For the Mittens and Stockings Garland we used inkpads, then colored the dots in with markers. The Christmas Light Garland was done with markers only. Stamp the Foam Core with as many images as you would like, depending on the desired length of your garland.

2. After the images have dried, cut them out with an X-Acto knife. Use the thick cardboard to protect your work surface. Change blades often to keep your edge smooth. Expect to go through a lot of blades.

3. Thread the embroidery needle with yarn, embroidery thread, or green dental floss. String the pieces by running the thread through the Foam Core from one side to the other at the top of each mitten, stocking, or light. Space the pieces 3" to 4' apart. If the pieces slide too much, put a small dab of glue where the thread goes into the foam to hold it in place. Tie off the ends with knots.

Hot Potatoes stamps used:
Mittens and Stockings Garland: Mitten #J412, Holey Stocking #J413
Christmas Light Garland: Christmas Light #F183

Velvet Wreath

Materials:

Hot Potatoes rubber stamp
(1/2) yard burgundy acetate/rayon velvet
(3) yards burgundy ribbon (1-1/2" to 2" wide)
(1) yard ivory satin ribbon (1-1/2" wide)
12" Styrofoam wreath
Straight pins with decorative "pearl" heads
Steam-A-Seam2 double-stick iron-on fusible web
Protective paper from the fusible web
Iron (no steam)
Misting bottle with tap water
Manicure scissors
Double-stick tape, glue, or pins for attaching bow
Scissors

Steps:

1. Follow the instructions on page 11 for Velvet Embossing™ with just one important amendment. Attach the Steam-A-Seam2 at the same time that you emboss the velvet. Simply place the stamp rubber side up on your work surface, and lay the velvet right side down on the stamp. Mist with water. Then put a piece of fusible web on the wrong side of the fabric, with a layer of the protective paper on top of the webbing. Use the area of the iron without steam holes to press over the protective paper for 10 to 20 seconds. This will emboss the image of the Poinsettia onto your velvet. The webbing will permanently bond to the velvet, making it more stable and also preventing it from fraying.

2. Emboss about 30 poinsettias on the velvet. Cut out all the poinsettias leaving a small edge of the unembossed velvet as the border for each piece.

3. Wrap a 12" Styrofoam wreath with 2" burgundy ribbon, overlapping it as you wrap to cover the entire wreath, and glue ends down.

4. Attach the poinsettias to the wreath form by inserting a straight pin through the center of each flower into the Styrofoam, overlapping the flowers as they are attached. The decorative pearl heads of the pins give extra punch to this wreath. Two rows of flowers cover the wreath nicely, 1 on the inside edge and 1 on the outside edge.

5. Use 1-1/2" satin ribbon to form the hanger for the wreath. Cut 1 piece of ribbon 18" long, and attach the 2 ends of the ribbon to the back of the wreath with straight pins, forming an inverted V. Use the remaining 18" of ribbon to make a bow and attach it to the top of the hanger with double-stick tape, glue, or pins.

Hot Potatoes stamp used: Poinsettia #T088

Patterns

Letter Holder - page 89

Enlarge pattern as desired

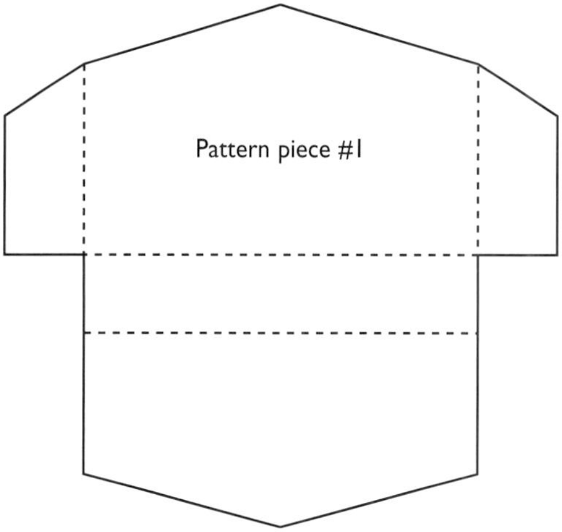

Pattern piece #1

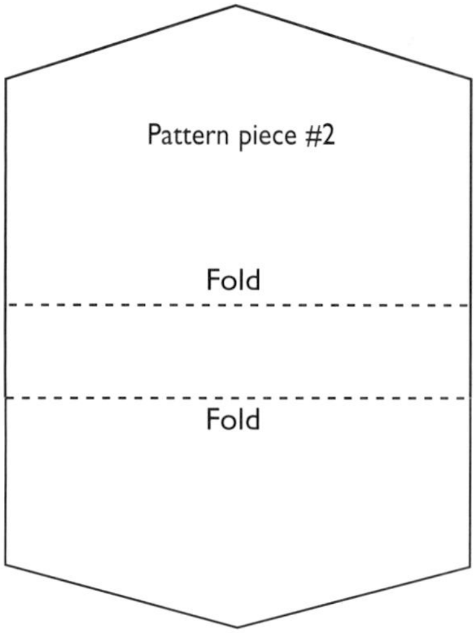

Pattern piece #2

Fold

Fold

Enlarge pattern - 400%

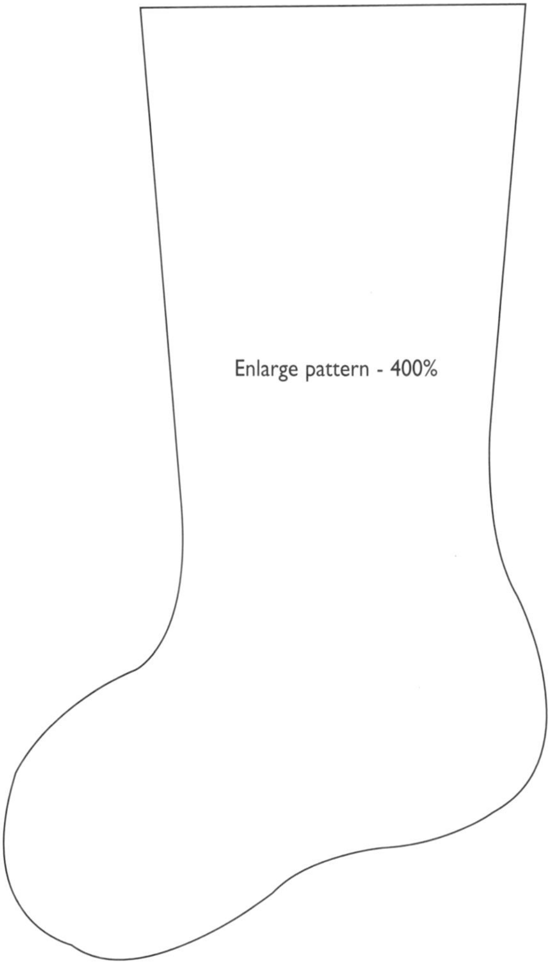

Bird Mobile - page 77

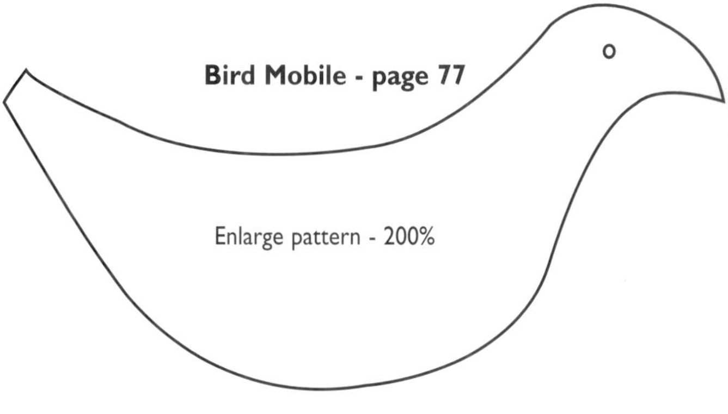

Enlarge pattern - 200%

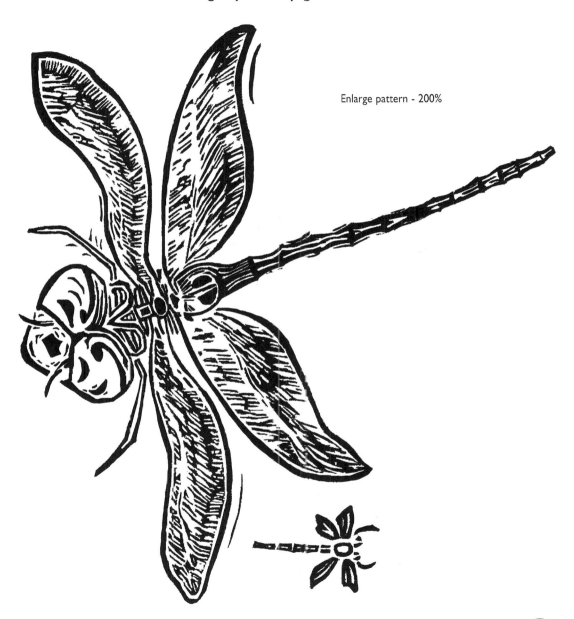

Enlarge pattern - 200%

Suppliers

Hot Potatoes Rubber Stamps
Phone (615) 269-8002
www.hotpotatoes.com
2805 Columbine Place
Nashville, TN 37204
Rubber stamps, Jacquard fabric paint, Res-Q Tape, Red Line Tape, Steam-A Seam2 fusible web, velvet by the yard, embossable velvet ribbon, Velvet Ornament Kit, Velvet Cornucopia Kit, velvet scarves and dye, Tile Kit, Resist Papers, foam brushes

Daniel Smith, Inc.
Phone (800) 426-6740
International (206) 223-9599
www.danielsmith.com
Safety-Kut Printmaking Block, linoleum carving tools, art papers, excellent catalog and fine art material source

Dharma Trading Company
Phone (800) 542-5227
www.dharmatrading.com
Textile markers, natural fiber clothing, huge selection of supplies for the textile artist

Textile Fabrics
Phone (615) 297-5346
4051 Hillsboro Pike
Nashville, TN 37215
Large selection of beaded and decorative trims, silks and other fine fabrics

Miscellaneous products may be found at your local fabric store and office supply store.

For specific rubber stamp supplies we encourage you to patronize your local independent rubber stamp store. Remember that the extra pennies spent at an independent store are rewarded with excellent customer service and individual attention. Please support your local retailer.

For a store near you, see the store listing on our web site www.hotpotatoes.com

If you liked our projects, you'll love this kit!

Hot Potatoes Velvet Ornament Kit

See special offer details on next page

The Hot Potatoes Ornament Kit includes instructions, prescored patterns and velvet squares to make 3 velvet ornaments.

You still need Hot Potato stamps, ribbon, tassels and adhesive and you'll be ready to please yourself or your friends with this great kit!

$12.95

Call us or mail in the coupon below

to receive a 10% discount off your Velvet Ornament Kit

Kit	$12.95
Less 10%	1.30
	$11.65
Freight	5.50
TOTAL	$17.50

Velvet Ornament Kit

Name _____

Street Address _____

City _____ State _____ Zip _____

C.Card#_____ Exp. Date _____
VISA/MC/DISCOVER

One per customer with original coupon

Hot Potatoes • 2805 Columbine Place • Nashville, TN 37204 • 615/269-8002
www.hotpotatoes.com • info@hotpotatoes.com